Where the Raritan Flows

D1564616

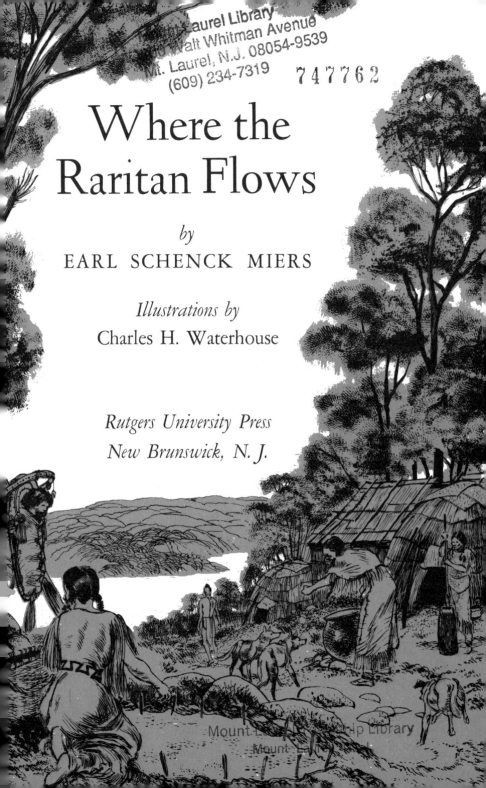

Where the Raritan Flows

by

EARL SCHENCK MIERS

Illustrations by

Charles H. Waterhouse

Rutgers University Press
New Brunswick, N. J.

To Charles Reed, with affection

The map on pages 146-47 was copied from a section of William Faden's map, "The Province of New Jersey," which first appeared in London in December, 1777. At that time Lord Howe's troops were resting in captured Philadelphia, while General Washington's men were enduring the rigors of the winter at Valley Forge and New Jersey was torn by guerrilla warfare between Patriot and Tory militia.

The map was based largely on surveys made in 1769 and was somewhat outdated at the time of publication. A second edition, issued the following year, incorporated some corrections based on observations of British and Hessian army engineers.

Originals of both maps are in the New Jersey Collection at the Rutgers University Library. The New Jersey Historical Society has published a color reproduction of the 1778 map.

Contents

Where the Raritan Flows

Chapter One

A Bird from Heaven

Crouched beside a bush, the Indian boy stared down at the river, his dark eyes wide with astonishment. Then the story his father told must be true!

There would come a day, his father said, when a great white bird would descend from heaven—a bird so strong, so powerful that if the bird flew away, it could carry fifty men on its back. The boy could not deny what his eyes beheld—there, floating on the glistening water of the river, was the great white bird.

The boy looked again, and still the bird spread mighty wings against a blue and cloudless sky. Crawl-

3

ing back from the bush, the Indian leaped up and turned so swiftly that he seemed like the deer he had been trained to hunt. He ran at headlong speed, bursting with excitement to describe the miracle he had seen.

The year was 1609 when Henry Hudson, exploring the coast of the New World between Sandy Hook and the entrance to the Hudson, sailed the *Half Moon* up the Raritan River. Indeed, there were men on the back of this "bird from heaven"—some twenty quarrelsome, unpleasant fellows who wished they never had sailed out of old Amsterdam. There is no record that the men from the *Half Moon* landed in the country we now call Middlesex County, and, considering their mood, that circumstance was a happy one.

For a time, then, while the Indian boy grew up and became a father in his own right, the land remained the domain of his tribesmen. His son, growing up, was taught many things: the legend of the bird from heaven, how babies must be cared for so that the evil spirit could not carry them off in unguarded moments, how to till the soil and plant corn and build a canoe.

Father and son tramped the great "Minisink Path" that ran from Navesink, near the entrance to Shrewsbury Inlet in Monmouth County, into Middlesex County. The path crossed the Raritan River at Kent's Neck, near Crab Island between Amboy and the mouth of the South River, then branched north-northwest across the Rahway River until it turned over the mountains west of Springfield and Newark. Still the

4

path stretched on, covering the length of Morris and Sussex counties and coming at last to Minisink Island in the Delaware River, below Port Jervis.

Any lad who traveled the Minisink Path learned to know the habits and strength of his people. In the high hills around Minisink Island he came to favorite hunting grounds where bear and deer and all manner of smaller game tested his skill with bow and arrow. As the weather grew warmer he dreamed of Navesink and the cooling breezes along the seacoast. He turned southward then, admiring the skill with which his ancestors had made this path cross every stream at the best fording place, traverse every swamp where solid ground existed, and ascend the easiest grades over hills and mountains.

When he reached the country we now call Middlesex and red shale outcroppings gave way to clay deposits, his heartbeat quickened, for he approached the seashore he loved so well. His days were busier here, for he was a good fisherman as the shell banks he left behind prove. Sometimes these cones of the shells of oysters, clams, and periwinkles rose to a height of twenty feet, and since such shells supplied the kind of wampum he valued, these mounds may be the waste product of one of the State's earliest forms of manufacture.

At heart this Indian was an easy-going fellow—a good parent to his children, a hunter who provided food for his family and pelts to keep his people warm, a tiller of the soil, a believer of romantic legends, a person of high intelligence. He was happy in this country the white man would soon buy from him.

The age of the Dutch settlements in the New World began in the early 1620's. Within a few years New Amsterdam, on Manhattan Island, became a bustling community of little black and yellow brick houses, each with a gabled roof, a fireplace in the kitchen where the family lived, a fat old burgher puffing on his pipe, a good wife busy at her spinning wheel, and a Negro servant perched, as Washington Irving wrote, "like a raven" in a corner of the chimney while she set the youngsters' scalps crawling with wild tales of Indian atrocities. Dutch settlers pushed across the Hudson into northern New Jersey, building little churches and trim farms and giving the Dutch name of Bergen first to a town and then to one of our northern counties. Southward they built a trading post along the Delaware River at New Amstel (New Castle, Delaware).

Faced with the necessity of connecting their settlements along the Noordt River (the Hudson) with those along the Zuydt River (the Delaware), the Dutch became the State's first European road builders. Their thoroughfares were simply paths for mail routes, sometimes traveled by white runners but more often by friendly Indians who passed letters from tribe to tribe.

The first road, most historians say, began at Elizabethtown. Here letters carried by ferry across the bay

6

started a long journey southward. Runners jogged through country that afterward became Woodbridge and Piscataway until they reached the ford across the Raritan at New Brunswick.

Eventually two roads were formed. The "Upper Road"—later called the "King's Highway"—marked the way through Kingston and Princeton to Delaware Falls (Trenton), thence across the river to Pennsylvania through Bristol to New Castle. The "Lower Road," branching off some miles west of the Raritan, wound through Cranbury to Burlington, where it crossed the Delaware and rejoined the "Upper Road" at Bristol.

What wonderful tales these runners must have told —of dense forests, of brooks and creeks where trout snapped at insects, of meadows sparkling with wild flowers, of rolling hills and valleys that echoed to sounds of distant waterfalls, of the flashing wings of game birds and the tracks of prowling wolves. Such tales, told and retold, became in time a call to adventure.

In August of 1664, four British warships appeared off New Amsterdam, demanding its surrender. Old Peter Stuyvesant, the governor, thrust two horse pistols into his belt, stomped his wooden leg, and called for a stout defense, but the principal response of his neighbors was the pounding of hammers as they nailed up their doors against the British invaders. So, "without a blow or a tear," New Amsterdam surrendered and the Dutch time in the New World ended.

Even before the new English masters divided New Jersey into East and West Jersey, an act in 1675 provided that "Bergen and the adjacent Plantations about them be a County," that "Elizabethtown and Newark make a County," that "Woodbridge and Piscataqua [Piscataway] be a County," and that the "two towns [Middletown and Shrewsbury] of Nevysink [Navesink] make a County."

These original counties—Bergen, Essex, Middlesex, and Monmouth—were defined more specifically "for the better governing and settling Courts in the same" by the General Assembly of East Jersey in 1682. This act designated Middlesex County as beginning "from the parting line between Essex County and Woodbridge line, containing Woodbridge and Piscataway, and all the plantations on both sides of the Raritan River as far as Chesquake [Cheesequake] Harbour Eastward, extending South West to the Division Line of the Province, and North West to the utmost bounds of the Province."

Six years later Somerset County was divided from Middlesex, for, in the judgment of the General Assembly, "the uppermost part of Raritan River is settled by persons whom in their husbandry and manureing of their land are forced upon quite different ways and methods from the other farmers and inhabitants of the County of Middlesex, because of the frequent floods that carry away their fences on their meadows, the only arrable lands they have, and so by consequence their interest is divided from the other inhabitants of said County."

The harshness of New England's winters, its grubby farmland, its constant religious bickering, among other causes, drove many colonists southward. Among these wanderers was the Reverend John Woodbridge of Newbury, Massachusetts, who gave his name to the oldest township in the county. The township itself was part of a vast tract of land, known as the Elizabethtown Purchase, bought in 1664 from three Indians for "20 fathom of trayden [trading] cloth, 2 cotes, 2 Gunnes, 2 Kettles, 10 barres of Lead, 20 handful of Powder, 400 fathom of white Wampom or two hundred fathoms of Black wampum."

An early description of Woodbridge sparkles with enthusiasm:

"Nature had furnished the country with all sorts of wild beasts and fowl, which gave them their food and much of their clothing." The following list must have whetted many a colonial appetite: "Fat venison, turkeys, geese, heath-hens, cranes, swans, ducks, pigeons, and the like. The streams abounded with fish, &c."

Nor was that all:

"Here you need not trouble the shambles [meat market] for meat, nor bakers and brewers for bread and beer, nor run to a linen-draper [cloth merchant] for a supply, every one making their own linen and a great part of woolen cloth for their ordinary wearing. Here one may lodge in the fields and woods, travel from one end of the country to the other with as much security as if he were locked within his own chamber, and if one chance to meet with an Indian town they shall give him the best entertainment they have, and upon his desire direct him on his way."

The charter for Woodbridge, granted June 1, 1669, stipulated that at least sixty families, "and as many more as shall be thought proper," must settle on the land and pay the proprietors an annual quitrent of a half-penny an acre. Settlers were entitled, subject to the Governor's approval, to choose their own magistrates, justices, and military officers and to send two deputies to the General Assembly.

Laws are not dull, for they speak of people and what is in their minds and hearts and dreams. So does this charter of 1669 speak when it provides that a majority of Woodbridge's settlers may "choose their own minister or ministers, towards whose support each inhabitant shall contribute according to his estate." Two hundred acres were set aside for the use of the minister and one hundred acres for the maintenance of a free school. Land used for a church or churchyard, a schoolhouse or market place was not to be charged a quitrent and a further guarantee was given to any inhabitant "of a different judgment in matters of Religion" to maintain a minister of his own choosing.

Punishments for crimes included "stocking, whipping (not exceeding twenty stripes), pilloring, ducking, branding, and the like," and no person was to be imprisoned for debt unless it should appear that he was about to defraud his creditors by leaving the country. Fines, when collected, were to be spent for charitable and public purposes.

The charter specifically guaranteed "liberty of conscience" and "free trade, unburdened by an excise or tax" except when such charges were imposed by the Governor or General Assembly to meet public debts. Inhabitants were expected to join with citizens from other towns in the event of Indian invasion or attack, but no warlike acts were to be taken without consent of the Governor, Council, and General Assembly.

By 1672 Woodbridge, a township of thirty thousand acres, supported one hundred and twenty families. A courthouse and prison were built and by 1695 there was a constable to collect taxes. Township officers were named for the duties they performed and so there were "meat-packers," "allowers of the town debts," "fence viewers," "lot-layers," "rangers." The keeper of the pound was an extremely important individual, for animals—especially horses, dogs, sheep, and cattle—could cause considerable destruction.

What manner of people were these early settlers of Middlesex County? John Bishop and Thomas Bloomfield were carpenters, John French a mason and builder, Samuel Hale a surveyor, Jonathan Haynes a cooper or cask-maker, Daniel Pierce a blacksmith, John Smith a wheelwright, Adam Hood a weaver. These men and women who cut down the forests of Woodbridge were self-sufficient, industrious, strong

11

in their faith in God, devoted to family. They had come here to endure, to prosper, to be happy, and their values reflected these wishes.

Thus the first Andros in the township, selling a lot of twenty acres, reserved for his wife's use "one peare-tree and some Gooseberry bushes," and doubtless Amy Andros enjoyed the fruit and berries to a good old age. Robert Dennis, willing his home to his two sons and his "two cows, five yearlings and all the movables in the house" to his daughter, stipulated that during their lifetime his children must provide their mother with the comforts of "meat and drink, washing, lodging and apparel." Hugh March came to the township, probably still grumbling over the scamps in Newbury, Massachusetts, who had persecuted his wife "for wearing a silk hood and scarfe."

A sense of order governed their lives. When in 1683 the tailor, William Toms, vented his anger by striking Rebecca Bishop, Toms received "thirty and nine lashes" at the public whipping post. For a "breach of his Majesty's Peace" the following year, William Ingle sat two hours in the stocks, and Otto Lowery was fined "for ranging the woods and marking a hors[e] contrary to the law of the province." Mathew Moore paid three pounds for speaking "against authority" and John Thompson, a Negro servant of Daniel Hooper [Cooper], was fined "for selling, giving, or other ways disposing of, so much rum to certain Indians as to make them drunk."

Elsewhere throughout the county, as other settlements took root, the people were much the same. Hugh Dunn, Hopewell and Benjamin Hull, John Martin, Charles and John Gilman, Robert Dennis, and John Smith, who came from Piscataqua in New England, gave that Indian name to the township they were authorized to establish on May 30, 1668, though the place soon was known as Piscataway.

Other sections of the township acquired local names reflecting the nature of the families who settled here. The pleasant stretch of farms along the road to New Market was called Fieldville in honor of the Fields family, whose founder came to America with Roger Williams in 1638. Rival factions of Baptists, settling around New Market and carrying on their old religious disputes, made that region known as Quibbletown or Squabbletown. By 1675 Piscataway was sending deputies to the General Assembly and by 1683 appointing its first overseers of roads.

Since so much of the township was fertile farmland, the conversations that filled evenings around the fireplace are easy to imagine—talk of cattle markings and how a swine's ear should be slit, clipped, or bored, of spring floods along the Raritan or Green Brook, of meadows that should be fenced and bridges repaired, of the town meeting house that was still unfinished in 1690 and the attention required by the stocks, the burying-place, the pound. Sometimes the settlers sat listening quietly for the howls of a wolf pack.

The place that the Indians called "Ompo" or "Ompoye," meaning "elbow," became on English tongues Ambo or Amboy. For more than twenty years after that August day in 1665 when Lord Carteret reached the province, the seat of government for East Jersey remained at Elizabethtown. But "Ambo Point" offered many advantages, even in these first years, to recommend it as the site of the chief town in East Jersey. A report in the early 1680's described it as "a sweet, wholesome, and delightful place proper for trade by reason of its commodious situation, upon a safe harbor, being likewise accommodated with a navigable river and fresh water, and hath, by many persons of the greatest experience and best judgment, been approved for the goodness of the air, soil, and situation."

By 1683 a "convenient town for merchandise, trade, and fishery" had made its start on Amboy Point. The three houses built that year were substantial structures for the time, each with a double chimney of wood and clay. About two hundred acres were laid out for the town and almost as many acres of salt marsh, three miles up the Raritan River, were set aside as a common pasture for the settlers. A survey of the harbor from Amboy to Sandy Hook disclosed a "broad and bold channel" and ships found safe anchorage even during "the hardest frost" of winter.

Events in Scotland were soon to have a decisive effect upon the new community. At the port of Leith on September 5, 1685, Richard Hutton, master of the

Henry and Francis, paced the deck of his ship. He took pride in a trim vessel of 350 tons, for she carried twenty guns and should prove a match for any privateersman she could not outrun. Aboard the craft now were about two hundred Scots, men and women who had been suffering the devil's own persecution for clinging to their "liberty of conscience" and who were determined to make a fresh start in East Jersey. Hutton wished these travelers luck, and they would need it since the voyage that followed lasted fifteen weeks. For a good part of that time fever ravaged the ship and as many as seventy probably perished before the December day when the vessel rounded Sandy Hook and dropped anchor at Amboy Point.

Those adults who could, paid five pounds sterling for their passage, and those who could not pay looked upon a country where they were supposed to be bound as servants to the proprietors for the next four years before receiving a bounty of twenty-five acres of land and a new suit of clothes. As freemen in mind and heart, if not in purse, they balked at such servitude and how many walked off is not known. Some settled in Woodbridge and Metuchen and others went to New England, but the influence of those who stayed was revealed in the frequency with which the town was now called New Perth, Perth Town or Amboy Perth in honor of the Earl of Perth, who had granted them refuge in East Jersey. The town was first referred to as Perth Amboy in 1692.

In 1686, the year when Perth Amboy became the

15

provincial capital of East Jersey, John Inian established his ferry near the ford where the old Dutch road crossed the Raritan. An earlier settler in New Brunswick was named Pridmore or Prigmore, and since a great part of the area was then a dense cedar forest and swamp the place was sometimes called "Pridmore's" or "Prigmore's Swamp." Some accounts say Daniel Hooper was the first inhabitant, and the name may be misspelled, for the Negro fined in Woodbridge in 1684 for selling rum to the Indians was a servant of a Daniel Cooper, then "living upon Raritan River."

In any case, John Inian—some records call him *Captain* John Inian—was the founder of New Brunswick, and for many years this tiny settlement was known as "Inian's Ferry." Inian was a man of judgment and initiative, serving both as associate justice of the court in Piscataway and in the councils of two provincial governors, and how long he ran his ferry before actually authorized to do so is anybody's guess. In time he paid the province an annual fee of five shillings for his franchise, so there must have been a profit in the enterprise.

Certainly the proprietors of Perth Amboy were well aware that Inian's Ferry existed, and to compete with the travel over the old Dutch road from Elizabethtown to the Delaware by way of Inian's Ferry, they opened a road between Perth Amboy and Burlington, the capital of West Jersey. A ferry crossed to South Amboy, providing the impetus for the settlement of that community, but the old Dutch road retained its popularity. By 1724, when somewhat belatedly Inian's Ferry became New Brunswick in honor of the ascension of the House of Brunswick to the throne of Great Britain, the settlement John Inian had started gave every promise of becoming the chief town in the County.

Six years later several families from Albany, New York, trudged down to Inian's ferry landing. Whether or not, according to Dutch custom, they carried their building materials with them is a matter of conjecture —perhaps they did. They liked what they saw, these blue-eyed, sober burghers who answered to names like Dirck Schuyler, Hendrik Van Deusen, John Ten Broeck, and Nicholas Van Dyke, and settling along the public road, they renamed it Albany Street. About this time James Alexander made a second visit to "New Brunswick at Inian's Ferry" and was astonished at the changes of fifteen years:

". . . when I came to this place in 1715 there were but four or five houses in the thirty miles between Inian's Ferry and the Falls of Delaware, but now the whole way it is almost a continued lane of fences and good farmers' houses, and the whole country is there settled or settling very thick; and as they go chiefly upon raising wheat and making of flour, and as New Brunswick is the nearest landing, it necessarily makes that the store-house for all the produce that they send to market, which has drawn a considerable number of people to settle there, insomuch as a lot of ground in

19

New Brunswick is grown to near as great a price as so much ground in the heart of New York."

In 1748, Peter Kalm, a naturalist traveling through North America for the Swedish Royal Academy, was no less delighted with the "pretty little town" situated in a valley on the west bank of the river. "The town extends north and south along the river," Kalm wrote, describing New Brunswick from a hilltop. "The townhouse makes a pretty good appearance. The town has only one street lengthwise, and at its northern extremity there is a street across. Both of these are of considerable length." Kalm, fascinated by the "Dutchmen" who lived along Albany Street, believed that "on the road from Trenton to New Brunswick I never saw any place in America, the towns excepted, so well peopled."

Kalm understood why New Brunswick prospered: "The greater part of its trade is to New York, which is about forty English miles distant. To that place they send corn, flour in great quantities, bread, several other necessaries, a great quantity of linseed, board, timber, wooden vessels, and all sorts of carpenter's work. Several small yachts are every day going backward and forward between these two towns. The inhabitants likewise get a considerable profit from the travelers who every hour pass through on the high road."

Almost a century and a half had passed since the Indian boy, crouching beside a bush, saw the bird from heaven gliding upon the Raritan. Now the country he had loved and called his own belonged to white men and was dotted by their farms and towns, crisscrossed by their roads, governed by their laws.

Some of their customs were good, some bad, some strange.

At Perth Amboy in 1729 the court found a Negro named Prince guilty of murdering William Cook, a white man. Prince was burned alive.

At Woodbridge in 1751 James Parker set up the first printing press in New Jersey and two years later published the *New American Magazine,* the State's first periodical.*

In 1712 Middlesex justices worried over a child named John Robison, whose ear was partly bitten off "by a jade [horse]." Concerned that the child might be suspected of having committed a crime meriting some such punishment as chopping off an ear as a sign of his guilt, the Middlesex justices issued a certificate "to prevent any scandal that he may be liable unto by strangers in any place where the providence of God shall cast him."

Such stories made exciting talk in Middlesex taverns, and they were stories repeated by post riders who carried the mails between New York and Philadelphia on alternate days "if weather permits"—at the standard rate, after 1764, of four pence for the first sixty miles, two pence additional for the next forty, and two pence for each one hundred miles thereafter.

* Probably the first printing for the county was done in 1723 for the proprietors of the Colony by William Bradford, whose print shop was located in New York City.

21

To use an Indian word, there was a "hubbub" everywhere—people on the move, meeting, talking, exchanging ideas. A distinguished visitor in 1774 was Massachusetts' famous statesman, John Adams, who wrote in his diary:

"Went to view the city of New Brunswick. There is a Church of England, a Dutch Church, and a Presbyterian Church in this town. There is some little trade here; small craft can come up to this town. We saw a few small sloops. The river is very beautiful. There is a stone building for barracks, which is tolerably handsome; it is about the size of Boston jail. Some of the streets are paved, and there are three or four handsome houses; only about one hundred and fifty families in the town."

Middlesex County had become a crossroads between north and south. Its citizens were alive to distant events, to changing thoughts. They knew, when skies darkened and thunder rumbled down the valley of the Raritan, that two storms were approaching—one in the heavens that heralded the coming of spring, another in the minds of men that might become a war.

Chapter Two

The Kings and the Liberty Boys

"The Kings are coming! Brace yourselves, my laddies! If it's a fight they want, we'll give them one they won't soon forget!"

The boy who spoke was a reddish-haired chap with the out-thrust chin of a brawling river boatman. As leader of the Liberty Boys, a band of New Brunswick youths who supported the cause of freedom in the first days after the war began at Lexington, he possessed a swagger that fitted the saucy angle of his cocked hat.

"There's nothing I hate more than Kings," the boy growled, slamming a fist into his palm.

The Kings, sons of Tories who believed that any uprising against George III was wicked and wrong, also could swagger, and thrust out their chins, and sniff on the April air the excitement of a good fight in the making. The rival bands came to a halt no more than ten yards apart. They exchanged insults and waved angry fists. Their faces reddened and their breaths shortened. The tension mounted until, unable to stand the suspense any longer, they went with a rush into the battle.

Blackened eyes and broken heads—too often a familiar sight on New Brunswick streets at the time—gave zest to the scuffle. The boys punched and kicked and rolled on the ground. Voices screeched. Adults, coming on the run, tried to separate the rival bands and might have proved more effective if they had not paused to exchange blows of their own. Eventually the fracas ended—out of sheer exhaustion, if the truth were told. Amid groans, both factions claimed victory.

By no means were hostile demonstrations between the Patriots and Loyalists of Middlesex confined to the youthful population. Quibbletown (New Market) had the case of Thomas Randolph, a cask-maker, who incensed his neighbors with his Loyalist sentiments. Randolph was stripped of his clothes, covered with tar and feathers, placed in a wagon, and ridden around the community for all to see until—or so a newspaper of the time declared—"he soon became duly sensible of his offence."

An obviously pro-British source in August of 1776 bewailed the fate of Donald Maclean, Theophilus Hardenbrook, Rem Rappalge, and young Feuter, the silversmith, all loyal to the Crown, for, this report said, they "have been cruelly rode on rails, a practice most dangerous, painful and peculiar."

And it was a long time before New Brunswick stopped chuckling over the schoolmaster who inflamed his patriotic young scholars with his Loyalist sympathies. Unknown to the schoolmaster, they pinned a sign to the back of his coat that read:"TORY!" The man walked through the streets while his students tagged behind, pointing and snickering, and he walked himself out of a job as well, for he was soon dismissed by the school.

The Revolution was like a fog settling over the Raritan, for all at once it was there—but even a fog can be predicted by a change of climate, a shift of wind. In like manner the Revolution was an event that grew in the minds of the citizens of Middlesex long before the first shot fired on old Lexington Common.

Perth Amboy might have its backsliders—men like William Franklin, the Royal Governor, and Cortlandt Skinner, speaker of the General Assembly—yet a New Brunswicker considered a traitor to the cause of liberty was hung in effigy on an October day in 1767, almost eight years before the war began. Two years earlier—in 1765—Middlesex's traders, merchants, and freeholders from Woodbridge to Kingston, putting on long faces and bobbing their wigs in anger, had been outspoken in resistance to the Stamp Act. And they did more than talk after the closing of the port of Boston as a result of the tea party in 1773—they formed Committees of Correspondence, writing letters about any infringement on their freedom and making common cause with sister colonies in exercise of their "liberty of conscience."

Stirring scenes resulted. Seventy-two delegates, representing every county, met in New Brunswick from July 21 to 23, 1774 for a general conference of the Province. A resolution condemned the British Parliament for acts that threatened the peace of the colonies and five delegates were appointed to the first Continental Congress to be held in Philadelphia that September.

The spirit of rebellion grew. By mid-January of 1775 delegates from the townships of Middlesex County were in New Brunswick for another convention. They came with resolute faces, sixty-nine delegates in all— from Woodbridge and Piscataway, from South Amboy and New Brunswick, from South Brunswick and Windsor (the latter two townships in Mercer County). As "freeholders and freemen of the county of Middlesex," they listened as John Dennis, clerk of the convention, read a resolution endorsing the acts of the first Continental Congress, saying in part: "We esteem ourselves as bound by the ties of virtue, honor, and the love of our country to contribute all in our power towards carrying into practice the measures which they [the members of the Continental Congress] have recommended."

A post rider, reaching New Brunswick at two o'clock on the morning of April 24, 1775, brought breathless news—British forces and the Minutemen of Massachusetts had clashed at Lexington five days before. So the war had come—a war, insisted patriotic Jerseymen, produced by the arbitrary acts of the British Parliament which made it "highly necessary that the inhabitants of this province be forthwith properly armed and disciplined for defending the cause of American freedom."

Events moved swiftly. General George Washington, en route to assuming command of the Continental Army at Cambridge, traveled through the county on June 24, 1775. The Commander-in-Chief had ridden out of Philadelphia the day before accompanied by Generals Charles Lee and Philip Schuyler. Rain had fallen that day, but Washington was cheerful if mud-splattered.

Middlesex hummed with war activity and every township echoed to the roll of drums as it raised companies of militiamen between the ages of sixteen and fifty. By voice vote each company chose its own officers—a captain, two lieutenants, and an ensign. Men who refused to bear arms were required to pay a forfeit of four shillings per month and it was a poor Committee of Safety that did not deal severely with anyone who neglected to pay his tax. Companies of Minutemen were organized and ordered to stand in readiness to march at a moment's notice to "the defense of this or any neighboring colony." Tar barrels and bags of feathers were set aside for Tories like Thomas Randolph of Quibbletown.

Fist fights between rival bands of Kings and Liberty Boys reflected the deepening uneasiness that developed. Neighbor often looked with distrust upon neighbor and in some families father and son were divided in their loyalty.

On that morning in 1776 when a post rider raced into New Brunswick, bringing a copy of the Declaration of Independence just adopted by the members of the second Continental Congress, many leaders in the county were frankly worried. Prudently they scurried to the home of Colonel John Neilson on Burnet Street, believing that disorder might be avoided if he, as one of the most respected men in the community, presented the Declaration to the people. As a landowner of substance, a merchant of wealth, a colonel of a battalion of Minutemen, Neilson was risking as much as anyone in supporting the war and Neilson left no doubt where he stood. There was only one choice, he said, "victory or slavery."

Still, Loyalist sentiment existed and a real question remained: Would the Colonel's prestige prevent an outbreak of fisticuffs when the Declaration of Independence was read in the market square?

With the first glimmer of daylight, farmers and their families began arriving. Quickly the stalls were filled. Children shouted and dashed between the legs of their elders. Men haggled over prices. A duck, escaping from the hands of its owner, waddled toward the river and women stopped gossiping as they watched a red-faced farmer chase down the squawking fowl.

Anyone listening that day learned much about the people who lived in Middlesex County during the lively times of the Revolution. Generally, they were a well-fed lot who took great pride in providing for their families. Householders boasted of how many barrels of pork or beef they possessed, how many sides of bacon, how many carcasses of venison and mutton. Their bellies made eyes sparkle on market day at the sight of a plump roasting pig, duck, turkey, or goose. They bargained stoutly for what they purchased, believing that "many a little makes a muckle," another way of saying "a penny saved is two pence clear."

They dressed comfortably. In summer the men wore breeches of linen or cotton fabrics like nankeen and white dimity and in winter their breeches were made of leather, buckskin, worsted and sometimes velvet. Dress coats and shirts, brightly colored stockings and calfskin boots and shoes added style to their appearance.

Gay colors were favored by the ladies in dresses and cloaks fashioned from materials like cambric, "taffety," Holland linen, calico, linsey-woolsey, muslin, and homespun. Bonnets and hoods varied among beaver skins, bright silks, satins, and velvets. The women spoke of their clothing with rugged honesty, describ-

ing a garment as "mostly new" or "half worn" or "the worse for wear."

They were, then, a people of simple virtues who valued most highly those things like food and clothing that were essential to their comfort and well-being. Was freedom with its threat of war one of those essentials?

That answer was to come as sunlight splashed over the market place. To the roll of drums militiamen went through their morning drill. The gossipers by now had heard of the signing of the Declaration of Independence, and so they were prepared for the appearance of Colonel John Neilson, a handsome figure standing tall and erect with his hair brushed back and his mouth straight and firm.

In a strong voice he read:

" 'We hold these truths to be self-evident, that all men are created equal, that they are endowed by their Creator with certain unalienable Rights, that among these are Life, Liberty and the pursuit of Happiness. . . .' "

A profound silence must have fallen over the market place. Colonel Neilson read on, listing the abuses by which the government in Britain had sought to destroy these rights. No longer could the colonies tolerate such acts—henceforth they were free and independent states.

" 'And for the support of this Declaration,' " Colonel Neilson concluded, " 'and with a firm reliance on the Protection of Divine Providence, we mutually pledge to each other our Lives, our Fortunes and our sacred Honor.' "

Cheers rocked the market place. Men sucked on their pipes and nodded wisely. Children hopped about as though freedom was a flea that had lodged in their breeches. Apparently those with Tory leanings slipped off to their homes.

Yet the Tories would have their chance to crow sooner than anyone expected. The loss of Fort Washington, across the Hudson from Fort Lee which also fell, now forced the Continental Army to retreat through New Jersey. Hard pressed by British troops under Lord Howe and Earl Cornwallis, General Washington and his ragged, disheartened soldiers reached the Raritan on November 30, 1776. They clattered into New Brunswick across the wooden bridge at the foot of Hamilton Street and townspeople watched grimly as flames destroyed that structure to slow down the British pursuit. Captain Alexander Hamilton rolled his cannon to the high ground near the present site of Kirkpatrick Chapel.

The Continental Congress expected Washington to make a stand on the banks of the Raritan, but the members of Congress had little understanding of the bedevilments that dogged Washington. New Jerseymen who he had believed would rally to his banner too often locked their doors and sat cowering by their fireplaces.

At New Brunswick the terms of service for the militia from Maryland and New Jersey expired and they didn't care how many Redcoats approached—*they* were going home! Washington pleaded with these militiamen, but, as he later wrote the president of Congress, neither the Jerseymen nor Marylanders "would consent to stay an hour longer." Rain fell next day when Washington, filled with gloomy thoughts, led his dwindling army down the road to Princeton.

Within another twenty-four hours the British and Hessians swarmed into the city—a cocky, boastful, thieving conglomeration, as the residents of New Brunswick discovered before the enemy's occupation of the community ended the following June. Cornwallis and Howe made their headquarters in the mansion of Colonel Neilson on Burnet Street and the Hessians occupied the Van Nuis house on Neilson Street. A log bridge replaced the structure Washington had burned and British forts were thrown up at the Landing and on the hills surrounding the city. Fields which now are the campuses of Rutgers and Douglass glistened with the tents of the invaders. Three regiments camped across the river.

Not all tidings depressed the patriots of Middlesex. Christmas night brought Washington's surprise attack upon the drowsy, beer-drinking Hessians in Trenton. No one was more upset by this event than Cornwallis, who had dreamed of returning to England for a vacation and found himself instead, on New Year's Day, riding the frosty road to Princeton in the hope of restoring order out of the chaos that Washington had left at Trenton. Rain pelted down in succeeding days, turning Jersey roads into sticky bogs and adding to Cornwallis's glum spirits as he sat out this foul weather in Princeton.

Meanwhile Washington's troops jabbed at the British in vicious little skirmishes that became a series of tricks by which Washington laid a trap. The Battle of Princeton, fought on the county's doorstep and lasting less than an hour, added to the humiliation of the confused Redcoats who retreated into Nassau Hall. Washington's boys lugged a cannon up to the college building, and after two or three volleys the British hung out a white flag.

"It is a fine fox chase, my boys!" cried Washington, in an exuberant mood.

Nor was Washington finished baffling Cornwallis. The Americans plunged back into Middlesex County and at Kingston were again on the road to New Brunswick. Cornwallis was certain that Washington intended to attack the British supply base at New Brunswick, and Cornwallis swore (if he was still in a mood to speak) that he was ready to deal a stunning blow. But at Kingston Washington branched off on another road that led him into the mountains around Morristown where, settling down for the winter, he could once more take satisfaction in the fact that he had outfoxed Cornwallis.

Yet the British also enjoyed triumphs. Washington's lieutenant, the remarkable General Charles Lee, brought to New Brunswick as a prisoner before being shipped to New York, supplied cause for conversation. Lee possessed scant respect for Washington, deriding him upon occasion as no "heavenborn genius." Perhaps this feeling explained why Lee had failed to hasten forward with the reinforcements Washington had so urgently needed in New Jersey.

Instead, Lee had moved at a snail's pace, not crossing the Hudson until the fourth of December and in eight days marching no farther than Morristown. Then he rested comfortably at a tavern in nearby Basking Ridge, where the British captured him in his nightshirt, writing a letter. Now in January of 1777 he was a prisoner in New Brunswick, doubtless still writing letters in his nightshirt whenever he got the chance.

That Tory rascal from Perth Amboy, Cortlandt Skinner, also was active as he drilled Loyalist sympathizers on Staten Island and played the game of setting Jerseyman against Jerseyman. A pamphlet of the time described Skinner as "the most ungrateful man in the world," explaining why: "Because he has joined the enemies of his country and enlisted men to fight against his neighbours, his friends and his kinsfolk; because he had endeavoured to transfer the soil that gave him bread from the rightful possessors to a foreign hand; and because, to gain present ease and transitory honors, he would fasten the chains of slavery on three millions of people and their offspring forever."

Skinner's Loyalist troops were known as "Skinner's Greens," and their raids into Middlesex made them thoroughly hated. On Bennet's Island, in the Raritan above New Brunswick, was an advanced garrison that bothered Colonel Neilson and his Minutemen. Snow fell on the night of February 18, 1777—it was no night for an attack—but suddenly Neilson and his boys loomed out of the darkness, overwhelmed the Tories, and captured the lot.

Yet whatever grim amusement the Patriots of Middlesex may have enjoyed at Charles Lee's downfall and the routing of the Loyalist garrison on Bennet's Island was small compensation for the hardships imposed by the British occupation of New Brunswick. Patriot and Tory sympathizer suffered alike. Indignant citizens in every community had tales of woe to tell of how the British and Hessians robbed their homes and often forced their victims to help carry away this stolen property.

Hay, oats, Indian corn, cattle, and horses disappeared in a twinkling whenever the raiders appeared, and, sick at heart over the scenes he witnessed, one shocked Loyalist recorded that "families were insulted, stripped of their beds with other furniture—nay, even of their wearing apparel."

Here are samplings of the losses suffered:

In *Woodbridge:* weather-boards stripped off a house, "2 Common Bibles, 1 Testament, and 1 Psalm Book," a "Negro boy 12 years of age," and "a new pare of Leather Britches."

In *Piscataway:* "650 Trees and Saplings cut down," "Wood for One fire for a picket of 25 men for 5 months," "1 clock without case, of the best kind," and "Two Skiffs, one a large new skiff, the other a small one."

In *New Brunswick:* a wagon and pleasure sleigh, "100 lbs. of Tobacco and a linen wheel," "2111 lbs of pork purchased that fall," and "25 dozen New England Scythes."

The list could continue for pages and cover every type of household article. Rare was the Negro slave who was not seized. Wine cellars were robbed systematically. Houses belonging to members of the militia, in the expressive phrase of Private William French of Piscataway, were "cleaned out."

Yet in time the British paid a costly price for this behavior as that short-tempered, disgusted Loyalist, Justice Thomas Jones of New York, realized:

". . . Not a stick of wood, a spear of grass, or a kernel of corn could the [King's] troops in New Jersey procure without fighting for it, unless sent from New York. Every foraging party was attacked. . . . The losses upon these occasions were nearly equal—they could be called nothing more than mere skirmishes—but hundreds of them happened in the course of the winter. The British, however, lost men who were not easily replaced; the rebel loss was soon repaired by drafts from the militia. It was of further service to the rebels; it taught them the art of war. It inured them to hardships, and it emboldened them to look a British or Hessian soldier in the face, whose very phiz would make a hundred of them run after the battle of Brooklyn and prior to the affair of Trenton."

Post riders from Philadelphia carried copies of Thomas Paine's new pamphlet, *The American Crisis*. "These are the times that try men's souls," Paine had written. Residents of Middlesex County believed him.

Chapter Three

Fighting for Freedom

Spring came on, warm and sunny. Like hibernating animals, the armies awakened to the scent of war.

At Morristown, Washington's skeleton force now had grown through new enlistments to almost 9,000, although desertions among old soldiers continued and discipline was slack. Since sooner or later the British at New Brunswick must make a move, in late May of 1777 Washington transferred his encampment to a valley near Bound Brook so that he could keep a sharp watch on the Redcoats.

Three forts were erected and cannon, mounted on a hilltop, stared down the valley of the Raritan. From "Washington's Rock," above Dunellen, the General had a clear view of his foes in New Brunswick. Whither did they intend to go—toward the eastern states or toward Philadelphia?

As a result of this game of cat and mouse, in early June, New Brunswickers witnessed the execution of an American spy. His name was Abraham Patten, and, according to Loyalist reports in New York, "at the Gallows he acknowledged all the charges brought against him." Patten was accused of offering a British soldier a bribe of fifty guineas if he would carry four letters to General Washington and General Israel Putnam, who was in command of a reserve force at Princeton. The Redcoat pocketed the money and delivered the letters to his own headquarters, thus dooming Patten, since the communications "proposed on a certain day to set Fire to [New] Brunswick in four Places at once, blow up the Magazine, and set off a Rocket as a signal for the Rebels to attack the Town."

The British opened a new campaign. On the night of June 13, old Amboy rumbled to the tread of 18,000 troops under Howe marching toward New Brunswick. Splitting his advance into two columns, Howe threatened Somerset Court House (today Millstone, and then the county seat) and Middlebush in the hope that by cutting off an American force at Princeton he could lure Washington from his hilly stronghold.

Guessing Howe's intention, Washington drew back his force from Princeton and refused to be led into a slaughter.

Howe's next ruse was to retreat toward New Brunswick in the expectation that Washington would come after him. For two days Washington watched, then yielded to temptation. A strong force under General Nathanael Greene, sent to harass the rear of Howe's army, advanced into Piscataway. Washington himself came down to Quibbletown (New Market) while troops under Lord Stirling, posted near Metuchen, guarded his left flank.

Howe now was ready to spring his trap and on June 26 made a sudden turnabout, moving in two columns toward Woodbridge and Bonhamtown. The British plan was beautifully conceived, for if Howe could swing around Stirling and seize the passes to Middlebrook, he would have Washington neatly cut off from the heights in his rear.

The sun beat down, for it was a scorching day. Scorching also was Stirling's temper, which was easily fired. Square-jawed and bull-doggish, Stirling stood his ground, parrying one thrust after another until he could manage an orderly retreat. Washington, hearing the gunfire near Woodbridge, quickly withdrew into the hills behind Middlebrook.

On June 30, 1777 the last of Howe's troops crossed to Staten Island and for the first time in eight months New Jersey and Middlesex County were rid of their cow-snatchers and clothes-stealers. Moods grew brighter, tongues looser, and Tory sympathizers harder to find. The war now moved southward with the battles at Brandywine and Germantown preceding the dreadful winter for Washington's shivering troops at Valley Forge while the British sat, warm and snug, inside Philadelphia.

Meanwhile the defeat of Burgoyne at Saratoga stiffened French confidence, resulting in their recognition of the American colonies as an independent nation. Tempers in London were short that winter of 1778 and somebody's head was certain to roll. The scapegoat became Howe, replaced in command by Sir Henry Clinton. With French naval and armed forces able to aid the Americans, Philadelphia was abandoned as a base in favor of New York, a port much more easily defended.

On June 18, 1778, the British crossed the Delaware and began a weary march across New Jersey through Burlington, Crosswicks, and Allentown so that they skirted the southern portion of Middlesex County as it exists today. Alertly, Washington gave pursuit, eager to stop Clinton and his army from reaching New York. The Americans moved in two columns along similar routes, going by way of Princeton, Cranbury, and Half Acre, then passing south of the county through Englishtown and Tennent.

At best the march was a misery for Clinton. The train of supply wagons that accompanied his columns stretched for a distance of twelve miles—a devilish hindrance considering that the British tramped over roads through dense woods. Doggedly, Clinton pushed on, cursing the militiamen of Middlesex and Monmouth who knocked down the bridges he must cross and felled trees across the roads. Above all, he cursed that string of wagons which now divided the middle of his forces.

Ten days later, as Clinton's Redcoats toiled down the road toward Monmouth Court House (Freehold), some five miles southeast of Middlesex County, Washington saw his chance. To Charles Lee, who had rejoined the Americans through an exchange of prisoners, Washington sent repeated orders: attack, ATTACK.

Lee bumbled the business badly, believing that his troops were no match for British Grenadiers, and Washington arrived to find his own boys taking the worst of the battle. Washington assumed command, and made the Battle of Monmouth one of his finest triumphs, leading Frederick the Great of Prussia to remark wryly: "Clinton gained no advantage except to reach New York with his wreck of an army."

New Brunswick's citizens cheered hoarsely when Washington marched into town, flushed with his victory at Monmouth. The campfires of his army lighted the banks of the Raritan for a distance of two miles. "We are now arrived in a delightful country where we shall halt and refresh ourselves," Colonel John Laurens wrote from his headquarters "on the lovely banks" of the river. "Bathing in the Raritan and the good things of the country will refresh us. I wish, my dear father, that you could ride along the banks of this delightful river."

Washington and his army remained in New Brunswick on July 4, 1778, the second anniversary of the signing of the Declaration of Independence. The town would not soon forget that joyous day. Washington and his staff reviewed the troops. Thirteen cannon, one for each colony, boomed in celebration and were followed by a running fire of musketry and the shouting of three huzzas "to the perpetual and undisturbed Independence of the United States of America." Soldiers adorned their hats with green boughs, warmed in spirit by the double ration of rum Washington ordered served in honor of the occasion. Youngsters pranced through the streets, shouting and singing and believing that never before had fighting for freedom been such grand fun.

Doubtless General Charles Lee was in another mood, for on this day in New Brunswick began his trial by court-martial for disobedience of orders at Monmouth. A second meeting of the court was held two days later. The trial excited the entire army and among Lee's harshest critics were Colonel Laurens, who liked bathing in the Raritan, and Alexander Hamilton, who had planted his cannon on the hill near Kirkpatrick Chapel during Washington's retreat through New Brunswick before the Battle of Trenton. Lee's case was continued wherever the army moved, and after Washington left New Brunswick—on August 12, 1778—Lee was found guilty.

The war drifted into other areas with British raids into Connecticut and a brisk little affair on the Hudson River at Stony Point. From November 28, 1778 to June 3, 1779, Washington spent a comfortable winter at Middlebrook, near present-day Bound Brook. There were gay parties in Pluckemin, where General Henry Knox and his fat wife stayed, and along the Raritan where General Nathanael Greene and his wife occupied the home of Derrick van Veghten. One of the two hospitals that Washington's army maintained that winter was located in New Brunswick under the command of Colonel Abraham Buford. Another spring saw Washington moving northward to West Point. But no matter where Washington went, as long as Clinton occupied New York neither New Jersey nor Middlesex County could rest in peace.

A memorable raid occurred on October 25, 1779 and the British culprits were the Queen's Rangers under Lieutenant Colonel John Graves Simcoe, a veteran of the war since the fighting around Boston in 1775. Amboy was first to hear the hoofbeats of Simcoe and his raiders after their nighttime crossing from Staten Island. Along the roads to Metuchen and Quibbletown (New Market) farmers awakened, hearing the horses racing by and thanking God that Simcoe and his Queen's Rangers appeared to have more pressing business elsewhere.

At Derrick van Veghten's home, where General Greene and his wife had passed the winter, the Britishers found several flatboats collected for the use of the Continentals. The bottoms of the boats were ripped open and the nearby Dutch Church burned. The hoofbeats turned presently along the road to Somerset Court House, where the courthouse made a handsome blaze.

Then Simcoe, riding hard through Franklin Township toward the crossing of the Raritan, was thrown from his horse during a spirited skirmish with Middlesex militiamen. Unconscious, Simcoe did not then know the remainder of that night's work—how his Queen's Rangers rode into New Brunswick, fighting the militiamen from street to street and sometimes from house to house. He did not then know how Militia Captain Peter Voorhees, losing his balance when his horse tried to jump a fence, was unmercifully beaten by the swords of the Britishers. He did not then know that the Presbyterian Church was fired—some accounts say "destroyed"—and that his raiders, sweeping back into Perth Amboy, crossed over onto Staten Island with small loss to show for their night's frolic.

Beside the road where Simcoe lay, unknowing of all this, a Middlesex militiaman raised his bayonet, wanting to put an end to this devil whose friends had murdered Captain Voorhees and whose raiders had disrupted almost the entire county in a single night. A hand reached out, stopping that fatal thrust —a hand belonging to Lieutenant James Schureman, a graduate of Queen's College (Rutgers) in the Class of 1775. Schureman by now was an old hand at war, a veteran who had served with the militia and the Minutemen and who had been a British prisoner both in New Brunswick and "Sugar House" jail in New York. One day he would serve New Brunswick as mayor and now he served his community as a soldier who would not kill a stricken enemy.

Simcoe was brought to New Brunswick where many citizens, angered at the death of Captain Voorhees, demanded the Colonel's life. But wiser advice prevailed, and Simcoe was hidden in a building at the corner of Albany and Neilson streets known for generations as "Washington's Headquarters." Later sent to a prison in Burlington, he was exchanged and captured again at Yorktown.

Middlesex County produced its own breed of daredevil raiders. Buccaneers at heart, these river boatmen swept down the Raritan to launch attacks on British shipping around Staten Island, Long Island, and Sandy Hook. One of the foremost of these hardy whaleboatmen was William Marriner, who kept a tavern along the Raritan and knew every river man for miles around.

A frequent visitor to Marriner's tavern was Captain John Schenck of the local militia and the sight of this pair with their heads together promised action. Too many New Jersey patriots were being held prisoner in the holds of British vessels to please their fancy—the situation called for bold countermeasures. Rounding up twenty-six friends, Marriner and Schenck set out from Matawan Creek on a June night in 1777. They landed near New Utrecht on Long Island, ran off with a number of Tories, and were back in New Jersey with the rising sun. Now they had prisoners to exchange—a risky game that they continued playing with the British in succeeding weeks. In time Marriner's luck ran out, and, captured and paroled, he returned to his tavern in New Brunswick.

But Marriner wasn't finished—not so long as his old friend, Captain Adam Hyler, would lead the Middlesex river raiders. Hyler—sometimes the name was spelled Hiler and Huyler—was a German-born sailor who reached New Brunswick at the age of seventeen. Some accounts say that he was once captured and forced to serve in the British Navy so that there was scant love lost between him and the rulers in London. At the outbreak of the Revolution, New Brunswick knew Hyler as a man of about forty who was comfortably fixed as the owner of a small fleet of sloops.

A gunboat, the *Defiance,* was Hyler's pride and it led his whaleboatmen on every raid. His crews were carefully selected, doubtless with Marriner's help—men who would take wild risks, who valued freedom above life, and who could pull a muffled oar at a steady twelve miles an hour.

Romantic tales were told of Adam Hyler's deeds. On an October evening in 1781 he left New Brunswick in the *Defiance* with two whaleboats in tow. Anchored inside the arm of Sandy Hook were five British merchantmen, a rich prize for any night's work.

A Royal man-of-war groaned at anchor close by and British shore batteries raised menacing guns. But Hyler and his boys knew their trade—they must strike silently, swiftly, skillfully. Suddenly the raiders boarded the vessels, plundering cargoes, setting fire to four of the merchantmen, and sparing the fifth only because there were women and children in the cabins. In fifteen minutes the raid was over.

Eight days later Hyler and his river-devils were back off the Hook, this time stealing two schooners and a sloop. On another occasion they blew up an eighteen-gun cutter after taking a considerable quantity of supplies and ammunition. When John Taylor, a tutor at the College who fought with the Middlesex Minutemen, was captured by the British and imprisoned in the Presbyterian Church, Hyler's raiders set him free within half an hour.

The Captain and his river men, knowing the twisting channel of the Raritan like the lines on their palms, easily outran pursuers. The splash of oars, mocking laughter fading on the night breeze, a muffled shout of "Heave to it, laddies, there's rum ahead," taunted British tempers until one icy January night in 1782 the Redcoats sent a sizable expedition to finish off Hyler, his crews, and his whaleboats.

Some three hundred British avengers came up the Raritan in several boats that chilly night. Toward midnight the barking of a watchdog awakened a farmer named Peter Wyckoff. Placing his ear to the ground, Wyckoff detected the measured stroke of muffled oars.

He dashed to the barn, mounted a horse, and became New Brunswick's version of Paul Revere.

From house to house Wyckoff shouted his warning of the approaching British. Lights twinkled in New Brunswick homes. Men came on the run, clutching their guns and pulling on their clothes.

The British were putting the torch to Hyler's whaleboats when the New Brunswickers stormed down. Guns flashed in the night and the town rang with angry cries. A running fight spread from street to street. From behind the walls of the Dutch Reformed Church, a spirited volley pulled the British up short. Soon the battle drifted back toward the river as the invaders scampered for their boats and the safety of Staten Island.

The British casualties were four killed and an unknown number wounded. The New Brunswickers counted their losses at six wounded (but none fatally), and another five or six carried away as prisoners.

The climactic campaign of the Revolution came in the summer and fall of 1781. British forces now operated in New York and Virginia, and General Washington, joining his French and American troops, planned a move against New York in order to relieve the pressure on his beleaguered army in the South. But mid-August brought news that a French fleet, sailing from the West Indies, would move to the entrance of Chesapeake Bay.

Washington saw his chance to outwit the British. If he could make the enemy believe he was preparing to attack New York while he marched his troops across New Jersey on their way to Virginia, he could strike a decisive—perhaps a fatal—blow at the British army there.

Surprise was essential to the success of Washington's strategy and not even the members of his personal staff were told of the General's intention as he started southward. The march through New Jersey was made in four columns—two American, two French. The Americans separated at Chatham, one column going by way of Bound Brook and the other taking the road through New Brunswick.

Washington reached the city on August 28, 1781. If his heart pounded with excitement he understood why—once across the Raritan it would be clear that he was moving on to Virginia. There must be no bungling now and Washington knew the very man who could help him. His name was Simeon De Witt (a graduate of Queen's College in the Class of 1776). De Witt had fought in the Battle of Saratoga before he was recommended by Governor Clinton of New York as a capable, amiable young fellow well qualified to serve the Continental Army as a geographer.

Dipping quill pen in ink, Washington addressed a letter to De Witt that revealed his secret:

"Brunswick, Aug. 29, 1781.
"Sir:—Immediately on the receipt of this you will begin

54

to Survey the road (if it has not been done already) to Princeton—thence through Maidenhead to Trenton—thence to Philadelphia—thence to the head of Elk through Darby, Chester, Wilmington, Christiana bridge.

"At the head of Elk [the debarkation point in Maryland for crossing Chesapeake Bay into Virginia] you will receive further orders. I need not observe to you the necessity of noting Towns, villages and remarkable Houses and places but I must desire that you will give me the rough traces of your Survey as you proceed on as I have reason for desiring this as soon as possible.

I am Sir
Yr very Hble Servt
Go. Washington."

Simeon De Witt must have executed his duties well, for the journey of the Continental Army proceeded to Virginia without flaw. The Battle at Yorktown that followed resulted in a complete triumph for Washington, and for all practical purposes, though the war dragged on three years, British resistance to American independence was broken.

When news of Washington's great victory at Yorktown set Middlesex County to ringing with cheers, it is doubtful if a single King remained to have his nose bloodied by a Liberty Boy.

The wounds of war healed. Slowly the colonies struggled toward nationhood. And the old Raritan, ebbing and flowing with the tides, played its own unique role in this wonderful drama.

Chapter Four

Steamboat Days

> On a shady upper deck,
>   Joined by friends so merry,
> Bless me! ain't it pleasant
>   Riding on the ferry?

This song, popular about 1840, belonged to an age when traveling by water was an American custom and to a time when competition among steamboats along the Raritan involved even the passengers, who held their noses in the air and refused to speak to neighbors who had journeyed up river on other craft. Rival crews, meeting in local taverns, exchanged raucous insults.

These wars along the river had their beginning in a bitter contest between New York and New Jersey over the right to control navigation on inland waters. When in 1790 Congress enacted a patent law, the nation was still so young that it had to find its way largely by trial and error. Unless an inventor could be guaranteed the exclusive use of his patent for a number of years, he could never hope to attract the large sums of money necessary to put his invention to practical use.

But was even this protection sufficient to insure the successful development of the steamboat? Apparently the legislature of New York did not believe so, for it granted first to John Fitch and then to Robert R. Livingston and Robert Fulton the sole right of steamboat navigation on New York waters. Fulton's *Clermont* made its famous run along the Hudson in 1807, thus providing a basis for the monopoly granted to Livingston and Fulton, yet three years earlier the gifted Stevens family of Hoboken had built and run a steamboat across the Hudson. In 1806 the Stevenses constructed the *Phoenix*, a steamboat designed to carry both freight and passengers.

Barred from New York waters, the Stevenses placed the *Phoenix* in service between Hoboken and New Brunswick. Black smoke pouring from her stack, the *Phoenix* proudly chugged up the Raritan, passing the slower freight-laden sailing sloops that filled the river.

Here was a new and exciting vision—the dawn, really, of a new era for the river and the county—but it was a sight that scarcely pleased Livingston and Fulton.

Quickly they retaliated by placing a new steamboat, the *Raritan,* into service between New York and New Brunswick and the first of the river wars started. The *Raritan* saved passengers the nuisance of ferrying to and from New York as they were forced to do if they sailed on the *Phoenix* to Hoboken, and the *Raritan* charged only one-third the fare of her rival. The *Phoenix's* owners knew that they were beaten and, deciding in 1809 to transfer the vessel to the Delaware, they at least had the satisfaction of sailing the first steamboat on an ocean voyage.

New Jersey tempers, however, had been ruffled. The monopoly that allowed only steamboats owned or licensed by Livingston and Fulton to operate in New York waters gave them, in effect, a monopoly over East Jersey waters. In 1811 the New Jersey legislature struck back with a decree that allowed a Jerseyman, whose steamboats were seized in New Yorks waters, to compensate for his loss by seizing any New York steamboat found in New Jersey waters.

Actually this 1811 decree brought Jersey-owned steamboat traffic on the Raritan to a standstill, for no Jerseyman relished running his vessels into waters where they could be confiscated. One scheme after another was tried to get around the legal blocks raised by both states, but no positive results followed. Then in 1819 a new figure entered the fight. Thomas Gibbons had been a prosperous planter in Savannah, Georgia, before changing his citizenship to New Jersey. Gibbons possessed a fiery temper, a good dose of pigheadedness, and a fat purse—all useful assets in waging a battle to the finish with the New Yorkers.

Gibbons was ready to run his new steamboat, the *Bellona,* from New Brunswick to New York by the summer of 1819. His rival craft, owned in New York, was a steamboat that bore the deceptive name of *Olive Branch,* for peacemaking was not an element in this affair. Gibbons announced that his fast-sailing *Bellona* would outrun the *Olive Branch* to New York by one or two hours. His fare would be half as much, including free transportation to and from the dock.

This river war produced finally one of the most famous cases argued before the United States Supreme Court. Gibbons' counsel was Daniel Webster, the best-known attorney in the country, and he must have pleaded capably for Chief Justice John Marshall ruled in his favor. Basic to the decision was the question: "What is interstate commerce?" Clearly the answer was commerce between two or more states, but not stopping at a state boundary. In interstate commerce, if the Federal Congress had acted, what authority had an individual state? In case of conflict between Federal and state interests, Marshall ruled, the Federal law prevailed. Thus in declaring the Livingston-Fulton monopoly unconstitutional, Marshall established forever the right of Federal powers to regulate commerce and navigation between states.

Tom Gibbons' victory boomed steamboat travel throughout the nation. Soon along the Raritan whistles tooting, bells ringing were a normal part of the day during "seasonable" weather. At the dock side, agents for rival stagecoach companies waited to snatch luggage and whisk passengers over the roads to Trenton where, nerves somewhat jangled, they could connect with steamers to Philadelphia.

Often agents boarded the boats and chalk-marked the luggage they would seize the instant the vessels nosed into the wharves along the Raritan. By 1832 the Camden and Amboy Railroad had drained off this passenger traffic, ending the cutthroat stagecoach days, but then this competition never had been anything more than a side show to the big show. There were mightier struggles to be fought along the river.

Passenger-fare wars became an old story on the Raritan. When in 1824 the New Brunswick Steamboat Ferry Company launched the *Legislator,* it attracted customers the first month by charging only twelve and a half cents for the passage to New York, then raised the fare to fifty cents. Promptly its rival steamers, the *Bellona* and *Thistle,* cut their fares to twelve and a half cents and a price war was on! Some twenty years later when the luxury steamers, *Raritan* (the second steamer so named) and *Antelope,* were battling for business on the river by each offering a fare of twelve and a half cents to New York, the *Antelope* threw in the inducement of breakfast served on board to all who wanted it. Then the *New Philadelphia* entered the competition, cutting the fare to six and a quarter cents. Apparently everybody won in this fight except the steamboat owners!

The *Raritan,* called the *Napoleon* before she was remodeled and launched in 1847, was the pride of the river. A reporter for the *New Brunswick Fredonian* could not disguise his delight with the vessel:

". . . Let us push our way down to the main deck. How ample, and beautiful! The saloon abaft the wheel —divided into two apartments for ladies and gentlemen—is truly rich and magnificent. Splendid mirrors, scarlet silk-velvet-cushioned mahogany divans and ottomans, and a chain of side-seats of similar description, adorn this beautiful apartment. A handsome marble-top centre-table, a beautiful article of light, neat, cane-bottom chairs, and the whole richly carpeted, constitute a prominent feature of this floating palace. The centre-posts, side-panels, and ceilings display richly carved gilt-work, emblematic of nature, music, and art. An oak-leaf wreath and vine particularly attracted our attention. Their execution is highly artistic. The windows of this saloon, thirty in number, are conspicuously, and with the greatest good taste, curtained with dark, transparent oil-paintings, representing a great variety of the most beautiful natural scenery in the country—such as views on the Hudson river, and in the eastern, middle, northern, western and southern states. . . ."

Nor did the splendors of the *Raritan* end here. There was a luxurious covered promenade deck, wa-

ter that was kept constantly cooled with ice, and "gentlemanly deportment, kindness and attention" on the part of all the steamer's officers.

Yet even in "luxury" the river wars went on. The remodeled *Raritan,* owned by the Napoleon Company of New Brunswick, soon met her match in the *Antelope,* owned by the Perth Amboy Steamboat Company, which added to its attractions two large paintings of Washington crossing the Delaware, the work of Henry Sanderson, a New Brunswick artist. Moreover the *Antelope* carried six hundred men and women from New Brunswick, South River, Perth Amboy, and other Middlesex County communities on a free excursion to Keyport—let the *Raritan* beat that service, if it could!

But hard luck followed the two steamers, for the *Antelope* collided with the *New Philadelphia,* with the captains of both vessels crying foul play and the *Raritan* caught fire and had to be beached on Bedloe's Island. In 1850 the *Antelope* was sent around Cape Horn to end her years of service in San Francisco Bay. The last of the great steamers of the Napoleon Company was the *John Neilson,* designed by Robert L. Stevens of Hoboken and named after the gallant colonel who in 1776 had read the Declaration of Independence to fellow townsmen in New Brunswick's market place.

Travel on the river could be vastly exciting. "The Raritan," wrote one passenger, "finds its sinuous way through broad green salt meadows that stretch off like soft carpets until they meet the clay beds and tangled woods of the Jersey shore. It was indeed Holland; the same flat landscape and long stretches of green marsh. One constantly expected a windmill to appear on the sedge, or the spires and crooked tiled roofs of a Dutch village."

In time railroad transportation doomed river travel, yet its romance lives on in the once popular song:

Back and forth from shore to shore,
On the rippling river,
Watching spray beads rise and fall,
Where the sunbeams quiver;
Reveling in the cooling breeze,
Every one is cheery;
Bless me! ain't it pleasant,
Riding on the ferry?

Along the old river today, sluggish and slumbering, stretch the remains of the Delaware and Raritan Canal. The weedy, neglected banks of its tow paths and its ancient locks long since have forgotten the lusty boatmen who once piloted their barges upon its placid surface. Forgotten also are the titanic struggle that went into building this waterway between the Raritan and the Delaware and the enormous part it played in the growth of the county.

Construction on the canal began in 1832. Gangs of Irish laborers, brought from New York, built shanties along the river. They dug and sang and drank and engaged in fist fights as the long ditch took shape under their swinging pickaxes and shovels. A cholera epidemic, late that first summer and fall, brought death to many of the workmen, but colder weather ended this contagion and by 1834 the job was finished. The freight carried over the Delaware and Raritan Canal during its first ten years of operation was disappointingly small to its owners, but gradually the situation improved and toll charges that in 1834 had amounted to only $11,064 by 1844 had reached $130,088 and by 1850 were $252,690.

The canal brought its own way of life to the county. This was a world in which people lived on a boat with two mules ahead and a rudder behind. A father served as skipper, his wife as cook, his son as deckhand. They were a self-sufficient breed, enjoying their independence, talking their own language. A "Chunker" was a person who hauled coal from the Pennsylvania region of Mauch Chunk, a "Skuker" a coal hauler from Schuylkill Haven. To "snub a boat" was to check its speed on passing through a lock.

On the Erie Canal with its low bridges a boat had to be a kind of Noah's Ark with its top knocked off, but on the Delaware and Raritan Canal, which had only swinging bridges, any respectable boat could navigate the stream "without scratching her paint." New Brunswick was the entrance to the canal. "Here," wrote a traveler in 1884, "are the company's offices, and just beyond is the first lock. The mule stables where the teams were kept, the boarding-houses for the men, and the grocery, hardware and fancy goods stores were together along the water-front."

At daybreak the river bustled:

". . . The boats ahead were arranged six abreast, the strongest among the loaded ones being selected to take the strain of the cables from the tow-boat. The rest fell in behind, the bow of each one being brought snug under the stern of the boat ahead and securely made fast. To prevent the tow from spreading, cables were stretched from the bow of each boat to the stern of its immediate neighbors, and so the whole mass was held fast, but with sufficient play to admit of easy motion when swung by the current or twisted by the tug. Here was a community which spent the summer months traveling. Germans, Hungarians, Canadian French, Pennsylvania Dutch, and Maine Yankees made up its population. At an early hour in the morning the families were eating their ham and eggs and sipping boiled coffee, seated with their children on the deck houses or the water barrels, or perhaps on the slanting hatches through which the coal is dumped into the hold. On one boat the woman was hanging out the wash, on another the men were mending harness and splicing the tow-ropes. The latter boat evidently came from some far-off point where the teams were not provided by the canal company, for it carried two big mules of its own in a huge box amidships. . . ."

Slowly this armada made its way up river to the canal entrance at New Brunswick. Here the boats took turns being drawn through the locks by means of a steam windlass. The mules waited along the path to be hitched to the vessels. Whips snapped and lines tautened. One by one the boats moved on.

An old canal dog usually lay on the boat deck, blinking at the sun. The tow-boy, who walked ahead, was not an imposing sight, for he looked as sleepy as the dog, his hair stuck out at all angles from under his slouch hat, and his shirt, trousers and cowhide boots were masterpieces of patches.

But he knew his job—everyone on the canal did. A good run the first day was fourteen miles and brought the boat to Ten Mile Lock, two and a half miles above Bound Brook station. For our traveler in 1884 it was a fascinating journey with a new adventure at every turn:

". . . From the high deck the canal seemed to be running up-hill, and the river much farther beneath than it actually was. The motion of the boat was like that of an Indian canoe well paddled. It is an ideal way to travel. . . . No dust, no noise, no hurry, no train-boy; stopping when you like; plenty of pure air; and for fresh vegetables you have only to run out a plank, and go ashore to the nearest farm-house."

Morning or evening, the refreshment of a cool plunge in the canal was no farther away than the deck rail. To nap in the sun again was a matter of desire, for man or dog. At evening there was always someone with a musical bent to offer entertainment— a good 'cello player perhaps, often a guitarist.

Another day's run brought the boatman to Kingston. He was in Jersey peach country now and he could see baskets piled high at the railroad stations, awaiting shipment to New York or Philadelphia. Afterward came the pretty journey through Princeton where for miles beautiful old trees cast shadows upon the water. Nearing Trenton, a boatman could always tell when he approached the state capital, for chemicals, mostly iron, discolored the water.

There was another unfailing aspect to life on the Delaware and Raritan. "The canal," our traveler in 1884 observed, "literally swarmed with boys of all ages, colors, and proficiency in swimming. They ran ahead of the boat, took a long dive, and came up in time to catch the tow-rope, or perhaps one would get astride of the rudder-blade, when instantly others plunged in, made a race for him, seized him and each other by any available limb, and hung on in a bunch or strung out in the wake with the boat under full headway."

Flour, grain, iron, limestone, lumber, and coal were the principal cargoes carried along the canal, but the wonders of what was aboard didn't stop there. Sooner or later along would come a boat full of potatoes, or another with a hold crammed with cheese, or bales of straw, or wooden chairs, until after awhile it seemed as though everything that appealed to the mind and taste of man traveled this waterway. So the canal was not only a world of its own kind of people but also of its own smells and sights and sounds as raucous mule drivers barked at their animals to "Slack up! Slack up!" or ranted at a barge in the way, "Git that blasted circus boat a-movin'!"

Today, except for the heavy freighters anchored off Perth Amboy, the life on the Raritan River consists mainly of speed boats bouncing over its sunlit surface or the husky rasp of a coxswain driving the Rutgers crew in practice on a spring day, and only the occasional splash of a youthful swimmer disturbs the year-long sleep of the old canal. Even in the age when both the river and the canal were booming, there was one lad in the county who dreamed of a time when man would travel by a better means. His eyes, like his dreams, were focused on the blue sky overhead.

Solomon Andrews
and His Airship

Middlesex County's forgotten genius is Solomon
Andrews of Perth Amboy. His *The Art of Flying*, published in 1865, is now an extremely rare book, and to
read it is to know a remarkable man whose ideas, if
they had been taken seriously, might well have shortened the Civil War.

Solomon's story begins on a drowsy Sunday morning
in Perth Amboy sometime during the middle of the

1820's. Then a youth of seventeen, he listened with only half an ear to the sermon preached by his father, who was pastor of the Presbyterian Church. Intently the youth's gaze followed through a window the flight of an eagle soaring overhead.

As Solomon watched the bird winding its way across the sky he sat up, to use his own phrase, as though struck by "an electric shock." Henceforth he possessed but one great ambition and that was to construct an airship that would enable man to control his flight in air as the eagle could.

Although in time Solomon studied medicine, he was earlier employed as a watchmaker. Anyone who watched Solomon handling tools quickly realized that this young man was a mechanical wizard. There seemed to be no limit to the range of his creative mind as in succeeding years he invented and patented a barrel-making machine, a sewing machine, fumigators, forging presses, velocipedes, gas lamps, and a kitchen stove. But Solomon's masterpiece during those early years was his "unpickable" combination locks, and they made him financially independent.

For that age, Solomon Andrews was also an advertising genius. There is a story of how in 1832 he placed a thousand dollars in a chest, secured it with one of his locks, chained the chest to a lamp post at the corner of Broad and Wall streets (then one of New York City's busiest intersections), and offered the money to anyone who could pick the lock. Many tried but no one succeeded.

Another account declares that in 1836 a locked safe was placed in the Merchant's Exchange while a large poster offered an award of five hundred dollars to anyone who could pick Andrews' lock. For two months various persons tinkered with the safe, but none could open it. Solomon sold his patent and returned to Perth Amboy thirty thousand dollars richer.

In Perth Amboy, Solomon Andrews found the old military barracks, built in 1757 and occupied by the British during the Revolution, fallen into ruins. Repairing the buildings and equipping them with various machines and engines, Solomon was ready for his next venture—the establishment of "The Inventor's Institute," a workshop where inventors could toil in happy, co-operative companionship. An advertisement in 1850 described the unusual institution that Solomon had built in Perth Amboy where seven buildings, arranged "in the form of a hollow square," included a keg factory, an engine house, a machine shop, a United States mail padlock factory, an office, and a wing "divided into eight distinct apartments for private workshops of inventors."

Solomon's dream of building an airship that would fly where man directed had not dimmed. The type of craft taking shape in Solomon's mind one day would be called a dirigible, and among the practical uses he would see for it was carrying mail and passengers between cities.

Let the scoffers laugh, if they liked—by 1849 Solomon was erecting in Perth Amboy a structure "like

73

a ship house" in which to build his airship. These were busy days as a framework 80 feet long, 20 feet wide, and 10 feet deep was suspended in the building. Thirteen thousand yards of silk, woven in China, was used for covering. Hydrogen, made by steam in five retorts set in a furnace, filled the bag. Solomon's flair for promotion did not fail him and the following advertisement appeard in New York newspapers:

"AIRSHIP. The public are informed that the Inventor's institute at Perth Amboy, New Jersey, will exhibit on the 4th of July next, and during that day only, the aerial Ship which they are now building, and which they hope to complete during the present summer. . . .

". . . The plan of the invention was laid 23 years since and has occupied the attention of its projector during that period. Tickets 50¢ each to admit a gentleman and a lady, every additional lady 25¢."

How many gentlemen—or "additional ladies"—attended the exhibit is not known, and doubtless all asked the same question: "Will it fly?"

"The vessel was never taken out of the house," Solomon Andrews admitted, a bit sadly, in *The Art of Flying.* "A small machine, about 12′ long, was filled and let go to the upper regions. It was sent toward the sea, and never afterwards heard from."

National events were to have their impact upon the workmen in the Inventor's Institute as well as elsewhere throughout Middlesex County. With the election of Abraham Lincoln as our sixteenth President, the threat of civil war hung heavily over many hearts. February 21, 1861, became an exciting day in New Brunswick. Vast crowds began early that morning to gather at the station of the Camden and Amboy Railroad, and Professor John C. Van Dyck, then a child five years old, perched high on the box seat of his family's carriage, later recalled: "I could see over the gathering, and I remember wondering in a childish way where all those people lived and who made all their hats."

Then the train chugged across the bridge, with snow blowing down onto the Raritan as the cars rumbled by, and the youngster's heart leaped: "How gay they looked! The cars were streaming with red, white, and blue flags and festoonings, the engine was wound about with bright ribbons, and even the trainman, who sat up in his little 'buggy' cover on top of the engine, holding the bell rope over the tops of the cars, had a flag wrapped around his hat."

There was a tremendous hurrah as the train came to a stop. Two men stepped onto the platform of the rear car—one the child's father, the other a stranger. The child remembered:

". . . A boy's father is always a big man to a boy. But that other man! What a giant he must be, I thought, for he was so much taller! He was dressed in long black clothes, had long arms and legs, a long face, and on his head a long silk hat. I couldn't help looking at him. He seemed such a very odd-looking man as he stood there taking off his high hat occasionally by way of bowing to periodic outbursts of applause. I do not remember what he said, if anything. He was there for only a few moments, and then the train moved off amid great shouts, the two men bowing from the platform until the train disappeared around a curve. The tall man was Abraham Lincoln. He was on his way to his first inauguration as President of the United States."

Thus, briefly, during Lincoln's lifetime, Middlesex County had one glimpse of its Civil War President. That April the Rebels fired on Fort Sumter in Charleston Harbor and the bloody years of conflict began.

A spirit of intense patriotism—a will to stand behind Lincoln and the Union, no matter what sacrifices were needed—swept across the county. Soon the *New Brunswick Fredonian* was reporting: "The price of American flags has risen four hundred per ct. within the last ten days; and bunting, which two weeks ago found few buyers at seven dollars a bale, is now hard to get at twenty."

Joyously the *Fredonian* told of "a man from East-Brunswick [who] dropped into a shop in this City to make some purchases on Monday afternoon and began to rejoice over the fall of Fort Sumter, saying he was glad of it, and hoped a company would be formed in this State to go and help the Secessionists break up the Union. This last sentence was too much for the patriotism of the shop-keeper, and the traitor had hardly got the words out of his mouth before he measured his length on the floor."

With equal fervor, the President of Rutgers told an audience that should the Governor of the State so wish "he can have one hundred able-bodied and able-throated men from Rutgers College on one day's notice."

In Perth Amboy nobody felt more keenly than Solomon Andrews the need to defend the Union. Putting aside his ambitions for building an airship, Solomon joined the Sanitary Commission, the Civil War equivalent of our modern Red Cross. In the spring of 1862 he was with the Union forces as they advanced onto the Confederate capital at Richmond. The fact that General Robert E. Lee finally beat back the northern troops and saved Richmond did not impress Solomon. In this campaign for the first time the Union had sent men aloft in balloons to spy on the position of the Rebels and the effort had failed because, in Solomon's opinion, the whole idea of how to employ aerial navigation had been wrong.

Andrews returned to Perth Amboy with his head throbbing with bold notions. On August 9, 1862, he wrote a letter to President Lincoln, suggesting his own scheme for using an airship in the war against the South:

"The plan is so simple that the cost will not be much more than that of a common balloon, but it will require secrecy to prevent the enemy from becoming acquainted therewith before our government shall have received its benefits. I have no doubt of being able to give it [the airship] locomotion in any and every direction, not only in calm weather, but against a considerable wind. As the best evidence of my confidence in the project, permit me to say that I am willing to pledge real estate now in my possession, valued at not less than $50,000, for the success of the undertaking. I will sail the airship, when constructed, 5 to 10 miles into Secessia [the South] and back again, or no pay. My cash capital is all invested in the padlock business and in a contract with the P[ost] O[ffice] Department, for U. S. mail locks and keys, or I would build the aerostat [airship] on my own account and present it to the government."

Lincoln never answered Solomon's letter. Next he wrote to Secretary of War Edwin M. Stanton, enclosing drawings of the proposed airship, and finally obtained an interview with an official connected with the War Department. The cost of constructing the airship was not the basic question—how, the official asked, did the inventor intend to direct his ship in flight? Solomon, remembering how the eagle had altered course by shifting its weight, answered simply: "By gravitation." The official walked away, baffled and unencouraging.

There was in Solomon Andrews a stubborn streak, and when the War Department heaped delay upon delay in approving his plan, his patience broke. "I intend," he announced on September 22 to the War Department and anyone who cared to listen, "to build one [an airship] immediately on my account, and if successful, I shall present it to the U. S. Government, in the hope that it may shorten the war."

In an accompanying letter to Secretary of War Stanton, Solomon described the type of airship he proposed to construct. His craft would consist of three cigar-shaped balloons, held parallel to each other. Beneath he would sling a small car so that its weight could be shifted at will from one end to the other. Thus, by shifting the center of gravity, Solomon, like the eagle, intended to govern the direction of his flight.

Official Washington brushed off his idea, not understanding it at all. On August 26, 1863, Solomon tried another letter to Abraham Lincoln, describing his airship as "ready for the final trial" and adding significantly: "I have not the slightest doubt that it can be more useful in crushing out this rebellion than five iron-clad [sea-going] vessels."

Solomon, of course, was thinking of the bombs that could be dropped on enemy concentrations and cities —he was, indeed, a man far advanced for his times. Nor had he lost his skill as a promoter as a headline in the *New York Herald* for September 8, 1863, would prove:

AERIAL NAVIGATION
An Extraordinary Invention—
The Air Navigated Successfully—
The Great Air Ships—Incidents of Their Trial Trips

The *Herald's* reporter made no secret of the fact that he had just witnessed "the most extraordinary invention of the age," describing the airship with its "three cigars pointed at both ends, secured together at their longitudinal equators, covered by a net, and supporting by one hundred and twenty cords a car sixteen feet below, under its centre."

Would the airship work? The *Herald* reporter wrote:

"On Friday, the 4th instant [September, 1863], he [Solomon Andrews] made his last experiment, and demonstrated to an admiring crowd the possibility of going against the wind, and of guiding her [the airship] in any and every direction with a small rudder having only seventeen square feet of surface. He made no long flight in one straight line, lest his modus operandi [that is, his method of steering] should be divulged; but by a most ingenious plan demonstrated her capabilities beyond all possibility of doubt, whilst he prevented a public knowledge of his method of propelling.

"After a few short flights, to satisfy himself and a few friends that all was right, and that she would do all he had contemplated, he set her off in a spiral course upward, she going at a rate of not less than one hundred and twenty miles per hour, and describing circles in the air of more than one and a half miles in circumference. She made twenty revolutions before she entered the upper strata of clouds and was lost to view. She passed through the first strata of dense white clouds, about two miles high, scattering them as she entered in all directions. . . ."

Solomon's airship was doing better than the eagle he had observed at the age of seventeen and the *Herald* reporter said humbly:

"As to her propelling power and motive apparatus, it behooves us not now to speak. It might be considered contraband of war, or affording aid and comfort to the enemy; for with such a machine in the hands of Jeff Davis, the armies around Washington would be powerless to preserve the capitol.

"We think Dr. Andrews deserves more praise for the patriotic ingenuity with which he has preserved his secret, and yet tried his experiment in the open air before the public, than even that manifested in the conception and construction of his machine. Of that and its beautiful simplicity we may have occasion to speak hereafter. We have the documents."

This report omitted some significant details—that the airship could carry three persons in addition to the operator, that its three cigar-shaped balloons had contained 26,000 cubic feet of hydrogen, that it had sustained a dead weight of 432 pounds. The *Scientific American* added: "The reporter doesn't mention Dr. Andrews descending, but we infer that he 'still lives.' "

Indeed, Solomon was very much alive—and discouraged. Letters from a number of persons who had witnessed the successful trial flight were sent to President Lincoln, apparently without much result. A long petition, sent "To the Honorable the Senate and the House of Representatives," led Solomon to write, somewhat bitterly: "The petition to the House could not be found one week after its presentation and reference."

Stubbornly pushing official Washington for an answer, Solomon finally secured a scientific commission to investigate his proposed airship. Capable people composed this commission—A. D. Bache who was superintendent of the U. S. Coast Survey, Joseph Henry who served as secretary of the Smithsonian Institution, and a major of Army engineers named H. C. Woodruff. "It is not impossible," this commission reported to the Secretary of War, "that he [Andrews] can really perform what he has asserted he can do."

Poor Solomon, going to Washington, could not even locate a copy of the report. Eventually he would hear that the Military Committee of the House of Representatives had considered his "aerial ship" and "after various discussions" had declined to recommend an appropriation to test its value. The Civil War was nearing an end and Solomon no longer felt any need to disguise his resentment toward the government:

". . . Surely it will not and cannot now be considered contraband of war to make an exposé of this invention to the public. The Executive Government has declined it. They have refused it even as a gift. The war is near its close. . . . And there is no reason why this invention should not be introduced for peace purposes in aid of the extinguishment of the enormous war debt. Its greatest value is for commercial purposes; and it must now be brought into use for the benefit of mankind."

Solomon Andrews never lost faith in his dream of that drowsy Sunday morning when, as a boy of seventeen, half listening to his father's sermon, he had watched the soaring eagle. Some day he would fly like that!

Did he?

The answer was in the *New York Times* for June 6, 1866:

"About 5 P.M. yesterday the promenaders on Broadway were astonished at the appearance of apparently a large fish sailing in the air about 1500 feet over their heads. The commotion along that great thoroughfare was tremendous. The usual calm sedate frequenters, with heads thrown back, were eagerly gazing skywards, and in consequence many collisions occurred. The fair sex seemed to become oblivious of the presence of the fashionable swells, and in their abstraction ran their sunshades into their eyes; while the gentlemen equally absent-minded played sad havoc with the hoops and other appendages of the perambulating milliner's frames and while the fish continued floating over the city it was nearly impossible to find a person who was not intently watching its movements; some even attempting to keep one eye on it and the other on the ground. All this commotion was caused by the second successful attempt of Dr. Andrews's Aereon, or flying ship, from the corner of Greene and Houston streets yesterday at 5 P.M. About that hour the Doctor, accompanied by C. M. Plumb, secretary of the Aereon Navigation Company, started on an experimental trip to test some improvements which were necessary in the rigging. About 100 persons only were present in the enclosure, but quite a mob was gathered outside."

Solomon Andrews's triumph had come at last—in this flight from Perth Amboy to Oyster Bay on Long Island he was flying where he wished to fly. Nor had he, judging by reports in the New York papers, lost any of his talent as a promoter, for as his airship passed overhead small squares of cardboard, floating down to earth, read: "Souvenir of her trial trip from the car of Andrews' Flying Ship."

Solomon's backers failed to share his intense faith in a dream come true and the Aerial Navigation Company was forced to close its doors. On October 19, 1872, the *Middlesex County Democrat* of Perth Amboy published a sad item:

"We are called upon today to chronicle the death of Dr. Solomon Andrews of this city which occurred on Thursday evening last after a sickness of about 3 weeks duration. The doctor had held many positions of honor and trust in this city, having thrice been Mayor, a[nd] frequently member of the City Council. He was Health Officer of the Port at the time of his death and had in many walks of life distinguished himself."

Yet had Solomon Andrews really failed? On July 4, 1912, Joseph Stewart, Second Assistant Postmaster General, addressed a letter to Dr. Edward E. Haines of South Amboy:

"The postmaster at South Amboy, N. J., is hereby

authorized to dispatch mails from South Amboy to Perth Amboy on July 4, 1912, one trip, one way, by aeroplane service, provided such mails be carried by a sworn carrier and without expense to the department."

A 40-horsepower engine, turning two chain-driven propellers, lifted the biplane with a roar on that day in New Jersey's first air mail flight. What Solomon Andrews had predicted, almost a century before, had come true.

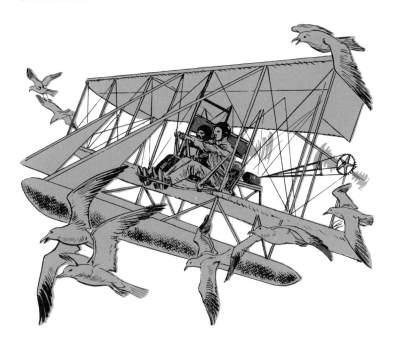

Chapter Six

The Old Dutch College

School days in colonial times were few and far between. Although the charter for Woodbridge in 1669 had set aside one hundred acres for the maintenance of a free school, twenty years passed before a town meeting decreed that James Fullerton should "be entertained as schoolmaster."

The indications are that by 1694 Woodbridge was still without a school, for early that year Jacob Brown of Amboy was engaged as a schoolteacher over the protest of a John Conger, who demonstrated his competence on the subject of education by signing his name with an "X." That November another gentleman, John Backer (or Baker), was engaged on a six-months trial to run "ye school this winter time until nine o'clock at night," which should have supplied him with a number of tired, restless young scholars on whom to exercise his birch switch.

The first school in Piscataway, taught by a teacher named "Gordon," was established about 1682, and Mr. Fullerton, who would subsequently offer his scrvices to the townsmen of Woodbridge, then conducted classes in Short Hills, near Plainfield.

Colonial Perth Amboy inherited peculiar problems. "Forasmuch as great inconvenience may arise by the liberty of printing in our said province," read early instructions from England, "you [the Governor] are to provide by all necessary orders that no person keep any press for printing, nor that any book, pamphlet, or other matters whatsoever be printed without your special leave and license first obtained."

Slowly the schools began—in Woodbridge, in Piscataway. The people who endured in a wilderness lived by their own wits, their own judgments, their own freedom of conscience. The Dutch families who came about 1730 from Albany to start life anew in New Brunswick belonged to this strong-minded breed. As other Dutchmen followed, their little churches and neat farms soon dotted the countryside. They became shrewd merchants, lawyers, doctors, craftsmen. They made busy housewives and stern papas and boxed the ears of youngsters who neglected to obey their parents. Family dynasties like the Voorhees, the Wyckoffs, and a dozen different "Vans" wrote their names into county records and the crumbling pages of forgotten newspapers. But their greatest monument would be the college—today the State University of New Jersey—that they began almost two centuries ago.

Of course the Dutch could not agree among themselves—in this respect, they were like the Baptists, who gave the name of Quibbletown to New Market. The warring factions among the Dutch churchmen were called the Coetus and Conferentie, and on the subject of the college they stood as far apart as possible. The Coetus wanted both a college of their own and the right to ordain ministers in the Provinces, whereas the Conferentie were against removing the power of ordination from Amsterdam and could see no sense in another college in the New World when King's College (Columbia) already existed in New York and the College of New Jersey in Princeton.

The argument quickly passed beyond the possibility of compromise. The church authorities in Amsterdam stood by the Conferentie—Dutch minds and purses, in those years, were never easily loosened—and tragedy was added to the controversy when Theodorus (Theodore) Frelinghuysen, who had pleaded the cause of the Coetus in the Netherlands, lost his life on the return voyage to Middlesex County.

A new leader in the struggle for the college became Jacob Rutsen Hardenbergh, who had studied for the ministry in the home of Theodore Frelinghuysen's brother. Now in his early twenties, Hardenbergh added vigor to resolution, though he had no better luck than his predecessor in winning support from the church authorities in Amsterdam. Yet Hardenbergh was pliable: if he could not secure a Dutch institution for the Dutch, then he would accept an English institution for the Dutch. A charter was granted by George III in 1766, but it was not until after a second charter was issued four years later, calling the institution Queen's College in honor of Charlotte, the Queen Consort, that Hardenbergh could feel victorious.

Meanwhile the Dutch had shifted their bickering to a new argument over whether the college should be situated in Hackensack or New Brunswick, and Hardenbergh, never one to lose a dispute easily, strengthened the New Brunswick claim by opening a grammar school in the fall of 1767. The young Dominie won his way, and in 1771 the first classes were held at "The Sign of the Red Lion," an old tavern that stood on the north corner of Albany and Neilson streets.

An early advertisement for the college offered to instruct students "in all the Arts and Sciences usually taught in public schools" so that they could become "a Pleasure to their Friends, and an Ornament to their Species." The troubled years of the Revolution followed, and, with the British occupying New Brunswick, classes were held for a time at Millstone and later at North Branch.

In 1786, Hardenbergh became the college's first president and a fresh start was made in a building where Monument Square stands today. Here classes were continued until the college was moved to Queen's Campus in 1811. As long as Hardenbergh lived, the college managed somehow to struggle along—true, often without paying the president's salary—but then Hardenbergh died, and the years for the college were filled with gloom and uncertainty. There was talk of a union with Princeton, a suggestion that may still curdle the blood of some Rutgers graduates during football seasons.

By 1825 the townspeople grumbled that the picket fence around the college property had become an eyesore, yet happier times were ahead due to a gift from Colonel Henry Rutgers, a New York philanthropist, and the name of the college was changed in his honor. The bell that still tolls in beautiful Old Queen's Building was another of the Colonel's benefactions. At its ring, students with long hair and stiff collars appeared for classes, moving a poet in later years to write:

> "And who was in the Catalogue
>   When College was begun?
> Two nephews of the President
>   And the Professor's son;
> Lord! how the seniors knocked about
>   The freshman class of one."

Doubtless they did, yet somebody also must have been knocking some education into the heads of the students, for Rutgers graduates were winning distinction in the world beyond the campus. Charles C. Stratton of the Class of 1814 became Governor of New Jersey. From the Class of 1836 Joseph P. Bradley became Justice of the United States Supreme Court, Frederick T. Frelinghuysen became Secretary of State, and William A. Newell became Governor of both New Jersey and the State of Washington. The Class of 1850 produced another Governor of New Jersey in George C. Ludlow, and the country's outstanding scientist of the nineteenth century was George William Hill of the Class of 1859 whose studies in celestial mathematics included the discovery of the moon's motion.

By the time of the Civil War the student body had grown to 124, and the desperate years had ended. Twenty-five undergraduates went off to fight for the Union and three for the Confederacy and only one, of all this number, returned to finish his education. The sadness at the death of President Lincoln was so complete that classes were suspended until after the President's funeral, but with time the wounds of the war healed and youthful energy found more normal outlets—in football and in a cannon war with Princeton.

It was inevitable that sooner or later the college and the river would blend together and that for generations Rutgers men would sing: "Take me down, down, down where the Raritan flows." The river, in a way, became the image of the college, for it was gentle and enduring and was filled with history and tradition.

If you will ignore a charge against a student in 1774 for the use of "a nine pin alley," the old river gave Rutgers its first organized sport in the spring of 1865 when a college crew rowed against a town crew. Baseball came along the following year, if you could call any game baseball when Rutgers lost an early contest to Princeton by a score of 40 to 2. Then on November 6, 1869 Rutgers and Princeton came together, with neither school completely knowing what it was doing, to create the American institution of intercollegiate football.

That first game, played on College Field in New Brunswick (site of the University gymnasium), certainly did not resemble football as we know it. Each team was composed of twenty-five players—two goal keepers, eleven "fielders" who guarded the home half of the playing area, and twelve "bulldogs" who carried the attack into enemy territory. Throwing or running with the ball was forbidden, there could be no holding of the ball or "free kicks" and "no tripping or holding of players."

Princeton's star was a rawboned Kentuckian named J. Michael, whom teammates called "Big Mike." For the Rutgers players—and for the Rutgers supporters perched atop a fence surrounding the field—he became a thorough nuisance before the afternoon ended.

Rutgers managed to score the first goal to the delirious joy of its rooters who, one newspaper said, burst into a cheer that sounded like "Ou! Bum! Haugh!" The Rutgers boys had driven the ball through the posts by using a formation not unlike the famous flying wedge of later years, and Big Mike glared menacingly as he saw the Rutgers players using the same maneuver. The Kentuckian smashed into the group, scattering the field with his rivals, and then, for good measure, crashed into the fence and toppled the spectators.

The Targum, Rutgers' undergraduate newspaper, reported afterward:

"To describe the varying fortunes of the match, game by game [each goal was called a 'game'], would be a waste of labor, for every game was like the one before. There was the same headlong running, wild shouting and frantic kicking. In every game the cool goaltenders saved the Rutgers goal half a dozen times; in every game the heavy charger of Princeton overthrew everything he came in contact with; and in every game, just when one of those delightful rushes at the fence was culminating, the persecuted ball would fly for refuge into the next lot, and produce a cessation of hostilities until, after the invariable 'foul,' it was put in straight."

The contest seesawed until the score stood at 4 to 4. Now Leggett, the Rutgers captain, called on his teammates to substitute strategy for brawn. The Rutgers boys, shorter than their Princeton opponents, needed only to keep their kicks low to have a decided advantage—or so Leggett believed. While Big Mike blustered and shouted and charged and panted, Rutgers quickly scored two goals and won the game, 6 to 4.

Despite the judgment of the editor of the *Bergen County Gazette* that the proceedings on College Field had represented "a jackass performance," football had come to stay. A second game played that season was easily won by Princeton, 8 to 0, and a third game was called off by college authorities on the ground that football interfered too much with studies. Rutgers would wait a long time before it again triumphed over Princeton. Then on a golden afternoon in 1938, in a game that officially dedicated the Rutgers stadium on the River Road campus, a sixty-nine-year-old jinx ended and the Rutgers boys were the victors, 20 to 18.

The old road to Princeton that Washington marched in 1776 and which Rutgers supporters travel each fall for the resumption of America's oldest football rivalry covers a distance of about seventeen miles. Down this road, at one-thirty o'clock on an April morning in 1875, rode nine Rutgers students in a farm wagon. Their raid that morning, the beginning of the Rutgers-Princeton Cannon War, would disrupt the county as it had not been disturbed since the days of Simcoe and his Queen's Rangers.

For many years—and particularly after the schools became football rivals in 1869—Princeton students had taunted Rutgers men with the story of how in 1859 they had taken a cannon from the New Brunswick campus. That cannon, boasted Princetonians, was now buried on *their* campus, and if the Rutgers boys had any spunk they would come and take it back.

The story was somewhat garbled, as legends usually are. It was true that the British had abandoned two cannon after the Battle of Princeton. It was true that, fearing an attack from a British squadron anchored off Sandy Hook during the War of 1812, New Brunswickers had borrowed the larger of these cannon and that the smaller cannon, a point of special pride with Princetonians, had been buried in the sand of a creek to keep New Brunswickers from taking it. The borrowed cannon was never needed, nor, despite repeated requests, was it returned to Princeton until a militia company, the Princeton Blues, marched off with the weapon and presented it to Princeton students as a souvenir.

By some wild stretch of the imagination, New Brunswick may have had a claim to the larger cannon, but the smaller cannon clearly belonged to Princeton. That April morning in 1875, however, the nine Rutgers raiders were not worrying over technicalities—the cannon they dug up and loaded onto the farm wagon was the smaller one (which, after all, weighed better than 1,100 pounds and nearly broke all nine backs to steal). By four o'clock the exhausted marauders returned to New Brunswick and dumped their prize on the grass before Old Queen's Building.

Tempers in Princeton soon reached the boiling point and, the *New York Sun* reported, Dr. McCosh, the college president, feared that "if his enraged students went to New Brunswick, bent on revenge, many of the two hundred and fifty students in Rutgers may be injured." Indeed, within a day Dr. McCosh was saying precisely this in a letter to the president of Rutgers, and adding significantly: "The cannon taken away never was at Rutgers College." Dr. Campbell, the Rutgers president, was no more anxious than Dr. McCosh to see heads broken, yet his reply revealed a note of stirred-up feeling:

"During my presidency of Rutgers College, no trophy shall be set up or continued on its grounds, of which the boast is made that it was stolen from any place. And now have I not the right to ask of you, in turn, the assurance that you will try to have the cannon, professedly stolen hence, returned? or, if there is no truth in this boast, that the falsehood shall be acknowledged?"

Princeton threatened legal action to retrieve the cannon, leading a local New Brunswick newspaper to speak its mind in no uncertain terms:

"Laird McCosh talks about the law, and darkly hints something about his young bantlings making a raid upon New Brunswick and taking back the cannon of contention. In regard to the law, we say let it take its course, and by the time the Supreme Court of the United States settles the matter the youngest Princeton freshman at this time will be as grey-headed as the oldest Princeton professor and as childish as the braggarts who talk about retaking the cannon by force."

Warming to this subject, the editorial writer had still more to say:

"In this city there are four thousand five hundred men over eighteen years of age, while the entire population of Princeton is less than twenty-eight hundred, including babes in arms, Princeton students, Dr. McCosh and other noncombatants of tender years and large ears. And a nice time they would have of it to come to New Brunswick and try and take that cannon back by force. At the first tap of old Rutgers' bell all the able-bodied men of this city would rush to the rescue, and the result would be that the Princeton 'stewed ducks' would all be ducked in the raging canal, while the belligerent laird would be put in a glass cage and exhibited to a wondering universe at five cents a sight."

By now there was not a hamlet, in Middlesex County or elsewhere, where partisans were not taking the side of Rutgers or Princeton. Editorial writers offered many suggestions for settling the dispute—one that the two schools hold a spelling bee to decide which should have the cannon, another that Dr. McCosh and President Campbell fight it out "in a twenty-four feet ring."

Finally a joint faculty committee from the two institutions ended the argument, but not before three wagon loads of Princeton students came to New Brunswick and attempted without success to find the cannon. The faculty committee sent the cannon back to Princeton, where it had belonged all the time, but the grief of New Brunswick and Rutgers in this decision was well expressed by an elderly woman who asked:

"Are they going to take that cannon back to Princeton?"

"Yes," came the reply.

"Well," said the woman, "they ought to be ashamed of themselves. If I had it I'd sink it in the Raritan."

Why this action hadn't been thought of previously is still the wonder of the entire affair.

Football games and a cannon war were incidents in the history of the old Dutch college—they were fun, but not part of the events changing forever the future of this institution.

It was not really by accident that in the years before the Civil War Perth Amboy produced Solomon Andrews and his Inventor's Institute, for both belonged to the driving force of an age in which America—and Americans—were changing. It was an age in which pride was taken in inventions ranging from the sewing machine to the magnetic telegraph. It was an age that released new sources of power ranging from the locomotives that traveled the tracks of the Camden and Amboy Railroad to the steamboats that sailed the Raritan. It was an age of oil wells, of new processes for making steel, of an awakening to industrial strength.

As far as education was concerned, that age achieved its goal when on July 2, 1862, President Lincoln signed the Land Grant College Act. By this legislation part of the land owned by the people of the nation—the "public domain" or still unoccupied land in the territories—was set aside to be sold for the use of a university within each state dedicated to serving the practical needs of that state's citizens. No longer were these institutions to be satisfied simply with emphasizing studies in Latin and Greek and theological subjects. They were also to teach science, to stress "agriculture and the mechanic arts," and to make education the servant of democracy.

Two years after Lincoln signed this famous bill, Rutgers became the Land Grant College of New Jersey and that fact, more than any other in the history of the old Dutch college, forecast the emergence of the modern university that now exists in New Brunswick. Two hundred and ten thousand acres of the public domain were set aside for the use of New Jersey and were sold almost at once for $116,000. This amount, held in trust by the State for the College, produced an annual income of less than $6,000, really not much to pay for the new responsibilities of education imposed by the Land Grant College Act, yet Rutgers faced the future in a hopeful spirit. A college farm, consisting of some ninety acres of land which had been the home of the grandsons of Jacob Rutsen Hardenbergh, was acquired for $15,000, and by 1865 courses in agriculture, engineering, and chemistry had been established.

The transformation from old Dutch college to modern state university proceeded slowly, and at times almost painfully. In New Jersey, as in other states along the Atlantic seaboard, many years passed before any real emphasis was placed upon agricultural education. Engineering, on the other hand, caught on at once, leading critics like President McCosh of Princeton to wonder aloud if money received under the Land Grant College Act was being used for its intended purpose.

If Dr. McCosh had read the act more carefully, he would have realized that the money was being employed quite properly—not only according to the letter of the law, but also in keeping with the spirit of an age when an industrial and professional outlook was beginning to dominate American life. Subsequently Congress increased the annual payments to all state institutions covered by the act, and in 1887 the Agricultural Experiment Station was established in New Brunswick.

By now Rutgers clearly was following its own path into the future. In 1890 the institution received its first state scholarships, and within the next twenty-two years new structures on the campus included a gymnasium, a library, and separate buildings for engineering, chemistry, and agriculture. The college belonged, as the county belonged, to a historic force that it might not always comprehend but which drove it nonetheless toward an inevitable destiny. A college for women, established in 1918, was another step in this direction. A ceramics building came two years

later, then buildings for specialized branches of agriculture—poultry husbandry and dairy husbandry—
followed in 1921. Thus science and the liberal arts,
as partners and friends, marched shoulder to shoulder toward that day in 1945 when all branches of
Rutgers University were incorporated into "the State
University of New Jersey."

The important point, then and in the future, was a
recognition of the fact that higher education belonged
to the people. Only the people can decide what the
university may be teaching a hundred years hence.
But Rutgers exists in the right environment today
because the county, like the country, has grown with
vigor and strength since those colonial times when
the Royal governors at Perth Amboy were cautioned
not to allow a printing press in Middlesex for fear of
what the circulation of new ideas could mean. The
college that grew out of a Dutchmen's squabble was
the symbol of the revolt that followed, for freedom
was in the air they breathed and the college was to
become the militant custodian of that freedom.

Chapter Seven

The Wizard of Menlo Park

No man better symbolized the forces of science and invention that were changing life in America than Thomas Alva Edison when he came to Menlo Park in 1876.

Edison now was in his early thirties and well on his way to becoming a national legend. The boy who had grown up in Ohio and Michigan, and who at the age of six had startled his parents by sitting on a goose egg in the belief that if a goose could hatch an egg, so could he, may have been the torment of his instructors but he was the delight of his schoolteacher-mother. She understood his inquisitive mind, his need to follow his own interests, the importance of allowing him to go his own way.

In the years when most youths were toiling over their lessons, young Tom Edison was earning his keep as a "newsbutcher" on the Grand Trunk Railroad. Later, as an expert telegraph operator, he exhibited the fascination with electricity that turned him finally to a career as an inventor. He tried without success to interest the United States Congress in an electrical vote counter, then scored his first triumph with a stock ticker. Edison, a modest young man of twenty-two, was determined to accept not less than two thousand dollars for this invention; it sold for forty thousand.

The Menlo Park to which Edison came in 1876 was a sleepy country village of a half dozen dwellings. The springtime quiet of the place delighted Edison—solitude and seclusion were fine for the "invention business." Close by was the railroad with New York City only twenty-five miles to the northeast. The spot seemed perfect.

In character, Edison soon had the village humming. Hammers banged and saws buzzed as workmen constructed his main laboratory, a two-story building thirty feet wide and a hundred feet long. Shortly a machine shop arose, then a glass blowers' shed, then a carbon shed for producing the lampblack carbon he finally used in the filament for his incandescent light. An office building and library joined this group of structures. In nearby Mine Gully a mile north of the village, an old copper mine, perhaps worked as early as Revolutionary times, was reopened. Tracks for an electric railroad eventually threaded their way through surrounding woods.

Meanwhile the dozens of experts Edison hired to work at Menlo Park seemed for a time to be arriving on almost every train. The dreams of Solomon Andrews for his Inventor's Institute at Perth Amboy were finding fulfillment under Edison at Menlo Park, and both operations, in their way, were forerunners of the gigantic research organizations now maintained by corporations like the Bell System and General Electric.

Edison was always a practical man. To him, inventing was a business and he wasn't interested in sweating over an idea unless he knew who was going to use it. In this spirit, his first important work at Menlo Park was devoted to perfecting the telephone.

The hundreds of Middlesex County residents who, along with millions of other Americans, attended the great Centennial Exposition in Philadelphia during the summer of 1876, had witnessed a demonstration of Alexander Graham Bell's new telephone. As a novelty, Bell's invention attracted attention, but hardheaded businessmen held reservations concerning its commercial possibilities. The range of transmission had been about two miles and even at this short distance speaking voices had been badly garbled.

The Western Union Company turned to Edison to

see what he could do toward developing a more efficient transmitter. Lights burned late at night at Menlo Park as Edison toiled over the essential problem of finding an apparatus which would transmit a greater degree of variation in sound waves. By March of 1878 Edison was ready to demonstrate that he had found the answer. One hundred and seven miles of telephone line were strung between New York and Philadelphia. The sounds came through strongly and men nodded, smiled, shook hands, and knew that the age of the telephone had been born.

Of his years at Menlo Park, Edison once said: "Everything succeeded in that old laboratory." With more than forty inventions being worked on at the same time, each under the charge of a different assistant, no one could deny that the "invention business" was thriving at Menlo Park.

The year 1877 supplies a good example of the variety of activity. In one part of the laboratory men worked on improvements for telegraph and submarine-cable devices. In another, technicians experimented with various types of telephones. In a third, workmen fussed over electric pens and mimeograph machines. In a fourth, experts tested sound-measuring instruments. In a fifth, scientists investigated chemicals and drugs.

Nor was that all. A crude incandescent lamp was made that year, but it burned out quickly and the idea was shelved temporarily. Meanwhile Edison was stumbling upon another of his best known inventions —the "talking machine" or phonograph. At the time Edison was working on a way to record telegraph signals, but his imagination never knew how to rest. Now it asked him: "If the diaphragm used in a telephone can transmit the voice, why can't the same apparatus record it?"

Edison began tinkering with a new machine, consisting of a disk with grooves that he could turn by hand. Tinfoil was placed over the disk and an embossing point, attached to a diaphragm, rested on the tinfoil. Edison's hope was that when he spoke through the diaphragm, the vibrations of his voice would be transmitted to the embossing point which in turn would trace those vibrations onto the tinfoil. By using another diaphragm perhaps his recorded voice could be played back.

Such was Edison's hunch when on a December day in 1877 he began to recite:

> "Mary had a little lamb,
> Its fleece was white as snow . . ."

The playback was perfect!

"What will you do with the machine?" a friend asked.

Edison shrugged his shoulders. He didn't really know.

For once Edison had misjudged the public—his "talking machine" became an instant hit. Newspapers, responding to the phonograph craze, began calling Edison "the New Jersey Columbus" and "the Wizard of Menlo Park."

Edison may well have regretted this feat of inventiveness, for the solitude of Menlo Park that he so treasured suddenly disappeared. Hundreds of visitors descended on the place. "They came," wrote a biographer, "from cities and farms, by carriage or wagon and train; indeed the Pennsylvania Railroad organized excursions bringing hundreds of persons at a time to flood the tiny hamlet that had grown famous overnight as 'the village of science.' It became the Mecca of a continuous pilgrimage of scientists and curiosity hunters. Foreigners arriving in New York by transatlantic steamer would ask their way to Menlo Park."

President Rutherford B. Hayes invited Edison to bring his phonograph to the White House. The two men talked until two o'clock in the morning.

For the next two years Edison worked steadily on the incandescent light. The problems were many— finding the right substance for a filament that would not burn out in a matter of moments, creating a near perfect vacuum since the presence of any degree of oxygen meant the filament would burn out rather than glow, developing a more efficient dynamo so that the electric current would be better distributed. At the same time producers of gas light systems in a number of cities were not above ridiculing the incandescent light as an impossible dream.

But Edison kept faith in himself. A newly developed pump enabled him to reduce the oxygen in his bulb to a fraction of a per cent of an atmosphere. He built a new dynamo, the "Mary Ann," and by using parallel connections devised a distribution system so that when one light went out it would not turn off all lights. Ten thousand different substances, ranging from platinum to human hair (and bright red hair at that, plucked from the beard of a friend), were tested in the search for a long-burning filament. Discouragement piled upon discouragement, yet Edison stuck to his search. At last he believed that he had found the answer in a strand of carbonized cotton thread.

Edison simply refused to sleep. He ate but rarely, and then nibbled at skimpy meals that should not have kept a bird alive. At any hour of the day or night the men in the laboratory at Menlo Park could be found working under Edison's relentless drive. By August they had reduced the amount of oxygen in a vacuum to one-hundred-thousandth part of an atmosphere—they had achieved the impossible—and for them to do so Edison had invented the glass globe into which such a vacuum was sealed, but that fact now was really a minor point.

The test of Edison's use of carbonized cotton thread came on October 21, 1879. For this experiment a piece of cotton sewing thread, bent into the shape of a loop or horseshoe, was sealed into a glass globe. The workers at Menlo Park could not disguise their strain, their expectations, their fears.

The dynamo whirred. Within the glass globe the carbonized thread glowed.

Edison's exultation bubbled over. "We've got it, boys!" he shouted.

And, indeed, Edison and his boys "had it," for forty hours later the piece of carbonized thread still glowed.

The men in the laboratory at Menlo Park stared down at that slender, fragile, brittle thread of carbonized cotton. They wondered why they had ever questioned Edison's ability to do whatever he said was possible. The man's reasoning power was without limit. He saw visions beyond the sight of other men— such a vision as they beheld now, looking at this glowing carbonized thread and realizing that it was the herald of the age of light.

The news of Edison's achievement became another sensation of the age. Once more the peace of Menlo Park was disrupted by the hordes of curiosity seekers who overran the little village. Some three thousand were there on the last day of December to welcome in the New Year of 1880 by having Edison demonstrate his most recent wizardry. A dozen lights were turned on and cheers rocked the quiet countryside. Later Edison gave another demonstration of his new miracle, using four hundred and fifty lights to illuminate a half dozen houses, the fields, the roads. One instant there was darkness, then at the flick of a switch Menlo Park burst into light. It was like magic.

One hardly could blame the curiosity seekers for

flocking to Menlo Park—it had become a place of marvels. By now the tracks for Edison's electric locomotive extended through the woods toward Pumptown, about two miles away. The engine, six feet long, consisted of a dynamo laid sidewise on a four-wheel truck. The laboratory's generating system supplied current through the tracks to the wheels of the truck and thus to the dynamo. In time the little engine was moving through the woods and around a nearby hill, pulling a coach loaded with fascinated spectators. If Edison had not built the country's first electric locomotive, at least he had built the best and largest electric locomotive the nation had yet seen.

The Edison Electric Company, created to finance his experiments with the incandescent light, turned next to electrifying a part of New York City. Soon Edison's presence was required throughout the country to supervise electrical projects and Menlo Park saw less and less of him. His family came back to the old house during the summer to rest and to enjoy the gently rolling hills, but after Mrs. Edison's death there from typhoid fever in 1884, even these occasional visits stopped.

Slowly Thomas Edison's part of Menlo Park fell into decay, its years of glory forgotten. The lower floor of the laboratory, where so many inventions had been conceived and perfected, became a cow barn. When in the early 1920's Henry Ford came through the place, seeking relics from the Edison period for a replica of the laboratory that he wished to build in his museum of industry and invention at Dearborn, Michigan, there was little to find. Ford reopened the shaft of the old mine in Mine Gully, but there wasn't much even here—simply an old hole in the ground in which Edison had buried his hope of extracting copper by an electrical process, one of his occasional failures. Ford's reconstruction of the laboratory at Menlo Park was opened in 1929, the fiftieth anniversary of the successful experiment with the incandescent light. Now an acknowledged genius and one of America's first citizens, Thomas Edison, then over 80, was at Dearborn that day.

Today the Eternal Light, burning on a hilltop at Menlo Park, honors the man who brought lasting fame to the county, and Raritan Township, of which the village is a part, has changed its name to Edison Township. The trains of the Pennsylvania Railroad, roaring along over electrified tracks, are a reminder of Edison's own little electric railroad that once wound through the woods toward Pumptown, and whose filling tank stood near Dismal Swamp at Metuchen. The light by which we read, the ring of the telephone, the sound of the phonograph are only a few of the means by which every day the magic of "the Wizard of Menlo Park" still touches our lives.

Chapter Eight

In the Steps of Weechqueechley

The tale is told of how, when the first settlers reached present-day Spotswood, they found a crude sawmill owned and operated by a half-breed Indian. How the mill came into existence is not known. If the half-breed built it, who taught him how? Or is it possible that some unknown white man, penetrating the wilderness of Middlesex County years before constructed the sawmill for the Indian? In either case, there stood the sawmill, powered by the waters of the South River and performing its work with reasonable

118

efficiency. For those who like romantic stories, it will do no harm to look upon the half-breed, whose name was pronounced Weechqueechley, as the county's first successful industrialist.

Surely Weechqueechley was a good symbol of how in colonial times the business life of the county depended upon products of field and forest. After 1715 the settlement of farm lands became rapid, a fact that exerted major influence on the region's industrial development. Fields of ripening wheat, rye, and corn soon produced a lively trade in grain and accounted for the gristmills that arose along the banks of the county's rivers, creeks, and brooks. Flour milling, an extensive enterprise by about 1730, in turn stimulated commerce on the Raritan and soon added shipbuilding to the list of industries. Carpenters, sawyers, and coopers were among the many craftsmen who found ready employment.

The old river, with its masted sloops and schooners, was like a magician's box that might open at any moment upon new surprises. The flood of German immigrants who in the 1740's settled in the upper valley of the Delaware came by way of the Raritan. These hardy settlers hauled their baggage by sloop to New Brunswick whence it was carted overland in wagons, and by 1757 a regular freighting service operated between New Brunswick and Bethlehem, Pennsylvania. Thirst produced its own industry and Henry Van Deursen's brew-house, which stood in New Brunswick before the Revolution, was described as a building seventy feet long and fifty feet wide with a malting cellar, a malt mill operated by horse power, and a vat capable of turning out twenty-two barrels of beer.

The romance in business is in the simple fact that it tells the story of the needs and dreams of people. The tanners, blacksmiths, shoemakers, and similar craftsmen who flourished in every community before the Revolution were kept busy because they belonged to their neighbors in this sense. So, too, did the post riders, and those robust rascals who drove the stage-coaches with a bounce that made teeth chatter, and the jaunty pilots of the ferry boats at Perth Amboy. The tavern keeper with gritty sheets on his beds served another purpose, after a fashion. However, he was a fellow on whom apparently a sharp watch must be kept and so in 1748 the Justices of the Peace of Middlesex County established standard tavern rates:

Prices of Liquors and Entertainments for Man, etc.:

	£	s.	d.
Hot Meal of Meat, etc.	0	0	10
Cold Meal Do [Ditto]	0	0	7
Lodging pr Night	0	0	4
Rum by the Quartern	0	0	4
Brandy Do	0	0	6
Wine by the Quart	0	2	8
Strong Beer Do	0	0	5
Cyder Do	0	0	4
Metheglin [fermented honey and water] Do	0	1	6
Lunch Do	0	1	2

And so in proportion for a larger or smaller Quantity.

Provision for Horses:

	£	s.	d.
Oats by the Quart	0	0	$1\frac{1}{2}$
English Hay pr Night	0	1	0
Do for 24 Hours	0	1	6
Salt or Fresh hay pr Night	0	0	8
Do for 24 Hours	0	1	0

And so in proportion for a Longer or Shorter time.

John Smyth, *Clk.*

Other needs produced other services. There were at least three fulling mills which finished the cloth woven in homes. And James Parker, setting up the county's first printing press at Woodbridge in 1751, demonstrated that there was also a thirst of mind for thought and information that must be quenched.

The Revolution changed America and within a generation the impact of these new forces was felt in the industrial life of Middlesex County. By 1790, Tench Coxe, who later would serve as an assistant secretary of the treasury, was telling the legislators of the State: "If New Jersey intends to maintain its proportion of respectability in the Union, Manufactures appear to be the principal means, for there are in the state but few vacant tracts of tolerable farming Lands." If New Jersey were really to prosper, Tench Coxe believed that it should fix its seat of government at a place "accessible by Sea, on account of coal, and foreign raw materials, and having a collection of people able to assist in the Business of Manufactures," and he

recommended New Brunswick, adding: "If any river in your state can be improved to accomodate the heart of it with internal Water Carriage it must be the Raritan."

Tench Coxe did not win over the legislators to making New Brunswick the state capital, but later events would prove him right in his conviction that the city contained "people able to assist in the Business of Manufactures." After 1778, when the county's courts were transferred to New Brunswick, the town was destined to become the leading commercial community in Middlesex. Early in the 19th century new industries appeared in the city—the tannery of Hardenbergh and Dunham, a paint works, a glove factory, and a large number of cabinet makers, tailors, builders of coaches and gigs, harness makers, and other artisans.

Cotton manufacture came next and brought a dyeing plant. A factory for iron and brass castings was another addition, and Captain McKay's pottery was hailed as "one of the largest and best conducted establishments of the kind in the United States." Burned in 1822, the pottery was rebuilt, and became famous for its manufacture of black teapots. A good brewery always depended upon an adequate water supply, and when in 1824 Levi Disborough (possibly Disbrow) succeeded in sinking a well to a depth of one hundred and sixty feet, distilling became a well entrenched industry.

The "Estimates of Rateables in New Jersey," comparing the years 1794 and 1831, reveal interesting facts about the industrial and economic growth of Middlesex County. In 1794 there were 172,128 acres of improved land in the county that by 1831 had grown to 185,337 acres and during the same period houses and lots of ten acres or less had increased from 490 to 1,257. Other comparisons were enlightening—for "horses and mules, 3 years old and upward," which had increased from 3,608 to 4,109; for "merchants and shopkeepers," which had increased from 45 to 108; for "sawmills," now 33 against 17, and "gristmills," now 51 against 42, and "tanyards," now 280 against 14. Of equal interest were the industries and businesses for which no count had existed in 1794 but which were taxed in 1831—fisheries, 4; snuff mills, 4; paper mills, 6; plaster mills, oil wells, and woolen factories, 2 each; cider distilleries, 39; toll bridges, 1; covered wagons, 92. The statistics were not dry when one saw the people behind them and understood the risks they were taking, the new needs they were trying to meet.

Up until the Civil War when access to the South as one of the best markets for snuff was cut off, the snuff mills played a special role in the industry of the county. The Brookford Snuff Mills, which operated in North Brunswick, was a good example of the enterprise. Four popular varieties of snuff were produced in this mill—"Scotch," "Maccaboy," "Lundyfoot" and "French Rappee"—but, far and away, the favorite was the yellow-leaf "Scotch." The tobacco used came largely from Richmond, Virginia, although purchases also were made in Missouri and Kentucky. Tobacco from New Jersey, like that from Connecticut and Delaware, was too light for snuff and was rarely, if ever, bought. Quality of product made the Brookford Mills famous and prosperous, both in wholesale and retail markets. The water power of Lawrence Brook turned its machinery and the enterprise might have gone on forever, had it not been for the War Between the States. Try as the proprietors did, they never recovered their market.

That historic events change business was a sad discovery for the owners of many of the county's snuff mills, but then gain as well as loss came from the same source. The year 1832 was a good case in point, for that year three of America's pioneer railroads were beginning operation—the Philadelphia, Germantown and Norristown Railroad in Pennsylvania, the New York and Harlem in New York State, and the Camden and Amboy line in New Jersey. The Camden and Amboy had a dandy little engine, the *John Bull,* imported from England and by 1832 had finished fourteen miles of track between Bordentown and Hightstown. But the Camden and Amboy always knew where it was going—it would follow the historic routes by which men had been crossing New Jersey for a century and a half—whether by steamer to Perth Amboy, then by rail to Bordentown, then by boat to Philadelphia (fare $3.00), or by a second route through Newark, Elizabethtown, and New Brunswick to Philadelphia (fare $4.00).

126

The coming of the railroad into Middlesex County, along with steam boat travel on the Raritan and the construction of the Delaware and Raritan Canal (see Chapter V), had a profound effect upon the business future of its people. Stagecoach days were over—and so, too, were stagecoach ideas. New thoughts, new capital rode the river, rails, and canal, and their influence upon the economic growth of Middlesex County would become enormous. The old Dutch, beating out their paths between New Amsterdam and New Castle, had foretold the future—these were the natural paths to the nation and the world.

So by river, rail, and canal the new industries came. The wallpaper factory of Janeway & Company (later Janeway & Carpender) grew into a New Brunswick institution. Nine printing presses, including one twelve-color and four eight-color machines, turned out millions of rolls of paper-hangings every year. Clay from Perth Amboy as well as from England and the South was used in mixing the colors. Velvet paper was made from flock—a French preparation of ground-up, colored woolen cloth—and water colors were printed by hand blocks. Gold and silver papers were other Janeway & Carpender specialties and each year the firm imported new designs from Paris, which in the second half of the 19th century was the wallpaper style center of the world.

The manufacturing of rubber products, including shoes and carriage tops, became another major industry. Some of the rubber pontoon bridges used by the

Army during the Mexican War were made in New Brunswick. The leading figure of this business was Christopher Meyer, who in time ran two factories in New Brunswick and one in Milltown, and who won the eternal gratitude of his neighbors by devising methods for eliminating the dreadful odors that were once part of rubber processing.

Other county industries by the 1880's included sawmills, buckram and mosquito netting manufacturing, a fruit jar company, an iron works, fruit canning, carpet making, several kinds of shoe manufacturing, a soap works, carriage making, cigar making, broom manufacturing, a toy rifle company, sail making, the production of wine sauces, the making of hats and caps, and a hosiery mill.

In addition, newspapers kept Middlesex citizens well informed. The county's first important newspaper was *The Political Intelligencer,* established by Shepard Kollock and Shelly Arnett in 1783. The *Brunswick Gazette* followed in 1786 and was succeeded by *The Guardian and New Brunswick Advertiser,* established by Abraham Blauvelt in 1792, with an editorial policy that stanchly supported the Federalists. The *New Brunswick Fredonian,* established in 1811, and the *New Brunswick Times and General Advertiser,* established in 1815, carried on a feud over Lincoln's policies during the years of the Civil War. The *Home News* was started in 1879 and other county newspapers then included the *Middlesex County Democrat* of Perth Amboy and *The Independent Hour* of Woodbridge.

The natural resources of the county stimulated other enterprises. The growing of apples and peaches became a chief agricultural pursuit and Washington (now part of South River) grew into a major shipping center with steamers leaving every day for New York. The clay deposits in the Woodbridge and Perth Amboy area produced such prosperous industries as the Salamander Works, established at Woodbridge in 1825 by Michael Lefoulon and Henry De Casse; John R. Watson's fire-brick plant, established at Perth Amboy in 1836; James Wood's brick kilns, established at Sayreville in 1851; and Alfred Hall's terra cotta plant, which was operating in Perth Amboy by the 1870's. Eight million bricks a year came from James Wood's kilns—this was big business. The bricks built the factories and the factories supplied jobs and the jobs brought people into the county. Large numbers of first-generation Hungarians and Poles settled near the industrial centers and proved to be efficient workers and good citizens.

Solomon Andrews building a better padlock in Perth Amboy, Thomas Edison perfecting the telephone and the incandescent light in Menlo Park, the old Dutch college in New Brunswick becoming the Land Grant College of New Jersey were each symbols of America emerging as an industrial giant. Middlesex County stood in the midstream of history. A proud past and a bright future carried the county into the 20th century.

Now, with more than six decades of that century

past, what is the image of the county's industry? The New Brunswick *Sunday Home News*, devoting several pages to a review of business enterprises in the county, quite properly calls the Raritan Valley "New Jersey's industrial parkland." Fine industrial plants that blend handsomely with the landscape are familiar sights on any Sunday afternoon's drive.

The range of business activity in the county is breath-taking. Orchids worn at state dinners in the White House frequently are grown in the greenhouses of Middlesex Borough. Near Cranbury, Creative Playthings, Inc., devises toys that can be used in the education of children. After one hundred and thirteen years of operation, the firm of Sayre & Fisher in Sayreville produces more than forty-two million bricks a year. In South Brunswick the Phelps Dodge Copper Products Corporation works on many processes involving copper in the nation's manufactures. In South River the R. & P. Wash Suit Company makes a million skirts and slacks a year for America's teen-agers.

And there are more: The Kilmer Museum of Surgical Products at Johnson & Johnson in New Brunswick, named for Dr. Federick B. Kilmer, an early pharmacist in the county and the father of the poet Joyce Kilmer, reflects the great contributions of this company to the health needs of the nation. After seventy-five years the Bey family of Woodbridge are still making barrels in the tradition of Abraham Bey of Perth Amboy, who started the business. Industrial jewels—used in gyroscopes, navigation instruments, missiles—are the specialty of the Moser Jewel Company of Perth Amboy. At the Forsgate Industrial Park in South Brunswick the Aeroquip Corporation produces more than fifty-five types of flexible hose and other apparatus employed in hydraulics, fuel, water, and lubrication applications for industrial equipment and heavy construction machinery. Heide candies—Jujyfruits, Jujubes, Diamond Licorice Drops, Darling Creams, Chocolate Sponge, and Licorice Pastilles—come out of New Brunswick.

And there are more: Edison produces backyard swimming pools, assembles Ford cars, turns out subminiature equipment for telemetry and computer uses, among other commercial activities. At Port Reading the Koppers Company plant, one of more than eighty of this company's plants throughout the country, turns out over one hundred and twenty-five groups of plastic products that serve more than forty basic industries. In Piscataway Township the research center of American-Standard concentrates on problems concerned with heating, plumbing, and air conditioning. In Plainsboro the Walker-Gordon Laboratory Company, now more than seventy years old, is the world's largest producer of certified milk (1,650 milking cows produce an average of 26,000 quarts of milk per day). In Dunellen the Bethlehem Steel's Buffalo Tank Division produces tanks up to a capacity of a million and a half gallons.

And there are more: in Parlin the Hercules Powder Company is one of the nation's largest producers of chemical materials for industry, and plants of the E. I. du Pont de Nemours & Company in Parlin and Perth Amboy carry on that corporation's tradition of "better things for better living—through chemistry." Dozens of other companies could be listed, ranging from the manufacture of prepared pie crust to research into new techniques for the Atomic Age. So stretches the procession that has followed in the steps of Weechqueechley, who built a wilderness sawmill on the banks of the South River.

A Postscript

Early on a Sunday morning I love to drive along the old river. As the rising sun sparkles on the water, the whole world seems fresh and clean and lovely. There is, in the quiet of such times, a wonderful sense of belonging both to the past and the future. One selects a spot along the river where trees jut out, and one thinks: "In some place like that the Indian boy stood when he first beheld Hudson's 'white bird' floating up the Raritan." One can still pick out the shallows that once must have been the fording places crossed by the first white intruders into this Red Man's domain.

The flash of a bird's wings revives history. Some

moment like this, the sudden upthrust of a fowl from the tall grasses, must have greeted General Washington as he led his weary patriots on their march to eternal glory at Trenton. The old Dutch college, then a decade old, came later to the banks of the river. Soon steamboats tooted their whistles and churned the water white with their husky paddlewheels. Then came the bawling, brawling canallers, these harbingers of a new age, a new economy.

One sees it all on a peaceful Sunday morning—the railroads that came, carrying Abraham Lincoln to Washington and a new birth of freedom for the nation, carrying Thomas Edison to Menlo Park and the fulfillment of the industrial revolution. One sees the factories that sprang up like toadstools along the river bank, luring later pioneers to a better life down where the Raritan flows.

A huskiness of throat is forgivable, viewing the old river then. Here I have lived and watched my family grow. Here I have loved. And here, in God's good time, I shall die and rest among my happy memories.

What's in a Name?

For the person who enjoys history there is no better sport than searching for the origin of names. True, this pastime is among the most baffling games on earth, and doubtless that master sleuth, Sherlock Holmes, would have been forced occasionally to admit failure. But even when the historian-detective cannot discover the devil who inhabited Devil's Brook in Plainsboro Township, or say for sure what settlers dwelt in the forgotten hamlet of Wigwam Grove, he has the fun of trying and there is always the exciting chance that one day he will stumble upon the answer. Meanwhile he has his share of triumphs and can mark "case closed" on why New Market was known as Quibbletown and whence came that fascinating name of Matchaponix.

Old Middlesex, with its long history, is a happy hunting ground for the historian-detective. His "clues" are many—old records and land deeds, local town histories, church records, faded newspapers, and a number of standard reference works of which W. Woodford Clayton's *History of Union and Middlesex Counties, New Jersey* is a notable example. Sometimes the memories of old residents can be helpful but they can also be faulty, and it will be a wise sleuth who weighs all the evidence before reaching a decision. Maps also help—the latest, the ones against which we checked, were published in 1960 and 1961—but no two maps include all the same names, or spell them all consistently. If the quest never seems to end, that fact demonstrates why the historian-detective is never lonely, for there is always something for him to do, some place to go, someone to see.

What's in a name? This question was perhaps the first I asked when I began this book. For over a year, assisted by William Miller of the history department of Rutgers University, the hunt has gone on. The rules of the game, as we played it, were simple.

We omitted as groups the names of old school districts, modern railroad and freight stations without historic significance, parks, and recent real estate developments. We did not expect to find every answer—

nor did we—and even though we had a source for every statement, we could not give an oath that we were not repeating someone's error of bygone years.

The result of our quest follows.

The first group includes names of townships, communities and neighborhoods still used by Middlesex mapmakers.

The second group gives names, now largely forgotten, of these same communities, so that the two lists can be used together.

We hope that others will take up the search and we wish them happy hunting. As a guide to their explorations, here is what we discovered:

A. TOWNSHIPS AND COMMUNITIES

ADAMS, in North Brunswick, once the township's only flag station on the Pennsylvania Railroad, probably derives its name from the Adams family which settled in the county in 1683.

APPLEGARTH, in Monroe Township, and settled about 1700, earlier was called "Spring Valley" and "Red Tavern." Anthony Applegate, who lived "near Red Tavern," was killed here during the Revolution by a band of men (presumably Tories).

AQUEDUCT, in Plainsboro Township, settled in pre-Revolutionary times, is named for an aqueduct by which the Delaware and Raritan Canal crossed Millstone River.

AVENEL, in Woodbridge Township, settled in 1901, is

137

named for Avenel Demarest, daughter of the community's original developer, and also was called "Demarest on the Hilltop." An Indian village in this vicinity was named Pocohant.

BERDINES CORNERS (BODINE'S), in North Brunswick Township, was settled in 1683 when Nicholas Bodine, blacksmith, brought his family here.

BLACK HORSE, in North Brunswick Township, derives its name from a tavern that stood on George's Road in the "latter half of the seventeenth century."

BONHAMTOWN, in Edison Township, honors Nicholas Bonham, who settled here about 1682. Early spellings also give the name as "Bonhamton." Five British regiments were briefly quartered here during the Revolution.

BROWNTOWN, in Madison Township, is so called because of the long residence in this neighborhood of a number of families named Brown, among them John and Susannah Brown who lived here in a log cabin in 1737.

CARTERET, in the northeastern corner of Middlesex County, honors the family to whom the Duke of York gave (with Lord Berkeley) part of his holdings in the New World west of the Hudson River. The borough was created in 1906 and known for a time as "Roosevelt."

CHEESEQUAKE, in Madison Township, is a name of uncertain origin. One theory suggests that the marshy grounds thereabouts resembled the "quaking bogs" in Ireland and another theory attributes the name to an early Indian village called "Chaquasitt," based on the word *cheseh-oh-ke,* meaning "upland." At one time the community was known as "Jacksonville" in honor of Andrew Jackson, seventh President of the United States.

COLONIA, in Woodbridge Township, may honor the Cone family, early settlers here. A previous name was "Houghtenville" or "Houtenville."

COLONIAL GARDENS, in North Brunswick Township, had its name chosen in a newspaper contest.

CRANBURY, a village founded before the Revolution (probably 1697), doubtless takes its name from Cranbury Brook. Its earliest settler on record was "Josiah Prickett, of Burlington." An early historian wrote: "When and by whom Cranbury brook was named is not known, and in former years it was often erroneously spelled 'Cranberry.' The name of the fruit cranberry is of Scotch origin. It was called 'craneberry,' from a real or fancied resemblance of its stem to the neck of a crane. . . . The old British custom, which our early fathers followed, was to call a district or town a borough, which was contracted into 'burg,' or 'bury.' When the village began to grow it was called Cranborough, or contracting it Cranbury." Until 1872 part of the present township of Cranbury belonged to Monroe and South Brunswick townships. See also *Wyckoff's Mills.*

DAYTON, in South Brunswick Township, was once known as "Cross Roads," because "five ways" or roads met here. During the Civil War, when Union feeling was strong, a movement was started to call the town "Lincoln." The name finally selected honored William L. Dayton, an attorney for the railroad who persuaded his company to assist the town in building a new schoolhouse. Dayton, nominated by the Republicans for the vice-presidency in 1856, later served Lincoln as minister to France and died in Paris on December 1, 1864.

DEANS, in South Brunswick Township, probably is named for Abraham Dean, who built a sawmill here in 1810. At one time the community may have been called "Martinsville," in honor of John H. Martin, a successful local merchant, and the *New Brunswick Sunday Times* for June 17, 1928, also refers to the original village as "Sandy Run." When a station was established nearby, the railroad selected the name of "Deans Station."

DUNELLEN, once "the extreme northwesterly part of Piscataway Township" and later divided from New Market by the tracks of the Central Railroad of New Jersey, has so many reasons given for the selection of its name that you may take your choice. One source says the name was derived from transposing the name of Ellen Dunn, an early settler. Another source believes that the town remembers Dunelleen in Scotland. A third source declares that Dunellen honors Edward Dunham, founder of the Seventh Day Baptist Congregation in New Market, and a fourth that it honors Dr. Dunell of New York, an early purchaser of property here. Other stories exist. Local residents long have preferred the Ellen Dunn story. The first settlers probably arrived between 1726 and 1735.

DUNHAMS CORNER, in East Brunswick Township, is named for Captain Jehu Dunham, a pioneer settler. His father was a settler near the Raritan, where Jehu was born.

EAST BRUNSWICK was founded by an act of the Senate and General Assembly of New Jersey on February 28, 1860, from parts of Monroe and North Brunswick townships. See also *Dunhams Corner, Hall's Corner, Herberts Corner, Monroe, Rhode Hall.*

EDGAR, in Woodbridge Township, honors the Edgar family, early Scottish settlers in the area. Captain Samuel Edgar of Woodbridge served in the Revolution and on June 11, 1757, Alexander Edgar agreed to contribute to the building of a bridge in Woodbridge.

EDISON TOWNSHIP, once known as Raritan Township, dates from March 17, 1870, when it was set off from parts of Woodbridge and Piscataway townships. The name, adopted in 1954, honors Thomas Edison. See also *Bonhamtown, Menlo Park, New Dover, New Durham, Nixon, Oak Tree, Piscatawaytown, Potters, Pumptown, Stelton.*

ERNSTON, in Sayreville Borough, may remember Otto Ernst, prominent in the mining of clay and sand in 1898. Ernst's clay mines were near the head of Cheesequake Creek.

FIELDVILLE, in Piscataway Township, owes its name to John Field who late in the 1600's settled on 1,055 acres of land along the Raritan between present-day Bound Brook and New Brunswick. In 1774 Michael Field was a delegate to the convention in New Brunswick that discussed the events leading to the Revolution. See Chapter II.

FORDS, originally known as "Ford's Corner," in Woodbridge Township, also was once called "Sand Hills" and "Slingtail Crossing." An early settler in the area was John Ford, who arrived about 1686.

FRANKLIN PARK, though partially in Somerset County, manages to poke a nose into North and South Brunswick Townships. It was once called "Six Mile Run."

FRESH PONDS, in South Brunswick Township, was the site of several fresh-water ponds in an area once known as "Pigeon Swamp." Other names were "Woodville" and "Woodside." Probably its first settler, about 1780, was Samuel Combs.

GRAVEL HILL, in Monroe Township, stands on high ground where the soil is still gravelly. A dozen old farm houses, with spacious grounds between, remain.

HALF ACRE, in Monroe Township, is of uncertain origin. An "Half-Acre Tavern" once stood here. One story insists that so many fights occurred in the place the village was called "the Devil's Half-Acre." Another story describes two roads that passed the hostelry, one in front and one in the rear. By fencing in the rear road, the original proprietor, Daniel

Lott, apparently left a half-acre enclosure behind his tavern for horses and carriages. Today two old houses and a gas station are all that remain of the settlement.

HALL'S CORNER, in East Brunswick Township, stands at the intersection of Cranbury Road (Route 535) and Rues Lane. The original Hall is unknown.

HELMETTA is a borough erected in 1888 and named in honor of Miss Etta Helme, daughter of George W. Helme, whose snuff-making plant is located here.

HERBERTS CORNER, in East Brunswick Township, stands at the intersection of Ryders Lane and Milltown Road.

HIGHLAND PARK, once part of Raritan (Edison) Township, was organized as a borough in 1905. Settled in 1675, it was formerly an Indian village known as "Falls of the Raritan."

ISELIN, in Woodbridge Township, described as "a post office" or a "post hamlet" on the New York Division of the Pennsylvania Railroad, also was called "Uniontown" and "Perrytown." Perhaps named for C. Oliver Iselin, a yachtsman.

JAMESBURG derives its name from James Buckelew, an early civic leader and benefactor. His father, Frederick Buckelew, leaving Scotland because of religious persecution in 1715, landed at Perth Amboy and moved to the Jamesburg area. James, born in 1801, died in 1869. The borough erected in 1887. The railroad station formerly was called "West's Turnout" (Billy West owned a tavern nearby), and for years conductors sang out both names—"West's" and "Jamesburg"—whenever trains stopped. Other early names were "Buckelew Mills," "Rossell's Mills," and "Ensley's Mills."

KEASBEY, in Woodbridge Township, recalls Edward Keasbey, president of the Raritan Hollow and Porous Brick Company, who settled in Perth Amboy in 1869 and organized the clay company in 1882. His brother, Anthony Q. Keasbey, served as U. S. Attorney of New Jersey, an office to which he was appointed by Lincoln in 1861.

KILMER, CAMP, a Federal military installation in Edison and Piscataway townships, honors Alfred Joyce Kilmer, New Brunswick-born poet and essayist best known for the poem "Trees," who was killed on a scouting mission during World War I. He is buried in France and received the Croix de Guerre.

KINGSTON, in South Brunswick Township, is a pre-Revolutionary settlement. Jediah Higgins settled near here as early as 1700 on 1,000 acres of land originally purchased from the Indians, and the Withington Tavern, built before 1776, was a main stagecoach stop. See Chapter II and Chapter IV.

LAURENCE HARBOR, on Raritan Bay in Madison Township, perhaps takes its name from that neck of land northwest of Keyport called Arewence by the Indians. At the mouth of Cheesequake Creek stood an Indian village variously known as Wromasang, Weomasing, or Ramesing.

LITTLE ROCKY HILL, in South Brunswick Township, is

described in old deeds with Kingston as a county boundary line. Washington marched through here after the Battle of Princeton.

MADISON TOWNSHIP was separated from South Amboy by act of the General Assembly of New Jersey on March 2, 1869. Named for James Madison, fourth President of the United States. See also *Browntown, Cheesequake, Laurence Harbor, Moerl's Corner, Morristown, Redshaw Corner.*

MAPLE MEADE, in North Brunswick Township, honors the Maple family, early settlers. A previous name was "Mapletown."

MATCHAPONIX, in Monroe Township, settled about 1700, is said to take its name from two Indian words —*Machtando,* meaning "devil" and *Ach-poan,* meaning "bread" or "poisonous root."

MENLO PARK, in Edison Township, is the site of the "Eternal Light," a tribute to the years Thomas Edison spent here inventing the incandescent light, among other modern miracles. See Chapter VII.

METUCHEN, a borough, derives its name from an Indian chief (Matochsegan) who, according to tradition, lived in this area between 1630 and 1700. The original Indian word means "high rolling hills." A pre-Revolutionary settlement, the present borough was organized in 1900 and a popular nickname is the "Brainy Borough."

MIDDLESEX BOROUGH was created in 1913. At a railroad station called "Lincoln" stands the original statue of Abraham Lincoln cast by Hubert and Alfonso

145

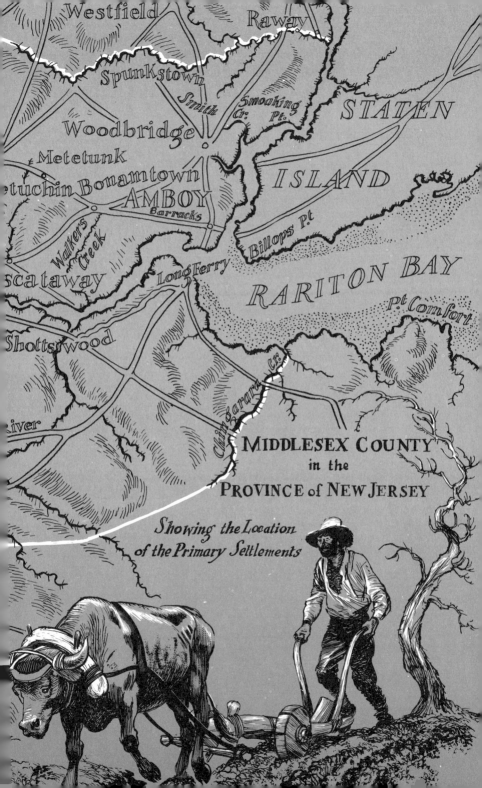

Westfield

Raway

Spunkstown

Smith

Smoaking
Cr: Pt.

STATEN

Woodbridge

Metetunk

ISLAND

tuchin Bonamtown
AMBOY

Barracks

Walkers
Creek

Billops Pt.

scataway

LongFerry

RARITON BAY

Pt Comfort

Shottsiwood

Cheesaquake Cr:

river

MIDDLESEX COUNTY
in the
PROVINCE of NEW JERSEY

*Showing the Location
of the Primary Settlements*

Pelzer. Duplicates of this statue—six in all—can be found in Ohio, Michigan, Pennsylvania, Nebraska, and Idaho.

MILLTOWN, south of New Brunswick and created as a borough in 1897, was the site of a gristmill owned by Jacob I. Bergen in 1800 when it was called "Bergen's Mills."

MOERL'S CORNER, in Madison Township, is probably a corruption of Morrell, the name of a once well-known family in this area.

MONMOUTH JUNCTION, in South Brunswick Township, takes its name as the juncture point for the New York division of the Pennsylvania Railroad and the Jamesburg and Freehold Railroad, connecting Middlesex County with Freehold, the county seat of Monmouth.

MONROE TOWNSHIP was separated from South Amboy by act of the General Assembly of New Jersey on February 23, 1838. The name honors James Monroe, fifth President of the United States. A portion of Monroe Township was given to East Brunswick Township in 1860 and a portion to Cranbury in 1872. See also *Applegarth, Gravel Hill, Half Acre, Matchaponix, Mount's Mills, South Amboy, Texas, Union Valley.*

MORGAN, in Sayreville Borough, derives its name from the Morgan family, early settlers near the mouth of Cheesequake Creek. Once famous as a vacation resort, the "Old Spey Inn" and its eccentric keeper, "Uncle Charley" Applegate, were especially well known. Ammunition, stored here during World War I, exploded on October 4, 1918.

MORRISTOWN, in Madison Township, may recall the first Lewis Morris who settled in nearby Monmouth County (Shrewsbury) in 1676. A later Lewis Morris became royal governor of New Jersey in 1738.

MOUNT'S MILLS, in Monroe Township, was once the site of a mill owned by the Mount family.

NEW BRUNSWICK, once called "Prigmore's" or "Pridmore's Swamp" and later "Inian's Ferry," adopted its present name about 1724 in honor of the ascension of the House of Brunswick to the throne of Great Britain. The county courts were transferred here in 1778. See also *Westons Mills* and Chapter I.

NEW DOVER, in Edison Township, may have been named for Dover, England. John Martin, a founder of Piscataway Township, came from Dover, New Hampshire.

NEW DURHAM, in Edison Township, takes its name from Durham, a cathedral city in England.

NEW MARKET, in Piscataway Township, once called "Quibbletown" and "Squabbletown," acquired its present name by 1834. Competing sects of Baptists, settling near here and carrying on their religious disputes, account for the earlier names. There is evidence that a miller once conducted a bank and a store here and that his establishment became known as the "new market place of Quibbletown." However, there is a New Market in England.

NEWTOWN, in Piscataway Township, was first called

149

"Randolphville," in honor of John Fitz Randolph, an early settler.

NIXON, in Edison Township, was named for Colonel Lewis Nixon, founder of the Nixon Nitration works and a designer and builder of United States warships.

NORTH BRUNSWICK TOWNSHIP, once part of Piscataway Township, was later referred to as "the North Ward of New Brunswick." The present title, used since 1803, included land now separately held by East Brunswick and New Brunswick. See also *Adams, Berdines Corners, Black Horse, Colonial Gardens, Maple Meade, Red Lion.*

OAK TREE, in Edison Township, is of doubtful origin. Obviously the "oak tree" existed somewhere and must have been a tree of impressive proportions.

OLD BRIDGE, in East Brunswick Township, was the site of the first bridge across the South River. After other bridges spanned this river, the town clung to its distinction as the place where the "old bridge" crossed. The community was once called "Herbertsville" in honor of General Obadiah Herbert, a prosperous businessman living here sometime between 1810 and 1840.

OLD CHURCH, in Monroe Township, recalls Anthony Applegate (see Applegarth), who, killed at home by a band of men during the Revolution, was buried on a nearby farm beside "two tall cedars." Early records, mentioning Old Church and Grove (perhaps Wigwam Grove) again are a reminder of David Brainerd, an Indian missionary in Monroe

Township. Close by is Union Valley where "Daddy" Perkins, a preacher who rode the circuit, organized a church class leading to the construction of a Methodist church in 1846.

OUTCALT, in Spotswood, was founded by John D. Outcalt, who built a snuff mill here about 1845. At one time it was known as the "Physical Culture City" because a magazine, *Physical Culture,* was published here from 1904 to 1907 by Bernarr Macfadden of New York. One story says the place was once called "Weechqueechley" because a mill, in pre-Revolutionary times, made that sound. More likely this name was derived from Weequahalaw, a half-breed who signed an early land deed.

PARLIN, in Sayreville Borough, was named by H. F. Brown, superintendent of the International Powder & Chemical Company and a descendant of the Parlin family.

PERTH AMBOY, called "Ambo" and "Amboy" by early settlers, and still later "the Town of Perth," eventually combined both names. See Chapter I.

PISCATAWAY TOWNSHIP derived its name from early New England settlers. The original spelling, "Piscataqua," was the name of an Indian tribe in Maine and also of a river that divided Maine and New Hampshire. See also *Fieldville, Newtown, New Market,* and Chapter I.

PISCATAWAYTOWN, in Edison, is the township's oldest settlement, dating from 1667 or 1668. An Indian village once stood here.

PLAINSBORO, in Plainsboro Township, was founded

about 1800. In the latter part of the 18th century, Matthew Griggs lived near here, and numerous Claytons and Davisons were later residents. See also *Aqueduct, Schalks, Scotts Corner.*

PORT READING, in Woodbridge Township, was a railroad terminus handling coal from Reading, Pennsylvania (which took its name from the English city of Reading).

POTTERS, in Edison Township, may remember James R. Potter, a member of the township committee in 1877. Also called North Edison.

PROSPECT PLAINS, in Monroe Township, was a station on the old Camden and Amboy Railroad. Early settlers were Cornelius Van Dorne and Henry Stults.

PUMPTOWN, in Edison Township, was settled in pre-Revolutionary times. A good guess is that an old pump, once standing in the middle of the road, was the source of its name.

RARITAN ARSENAL, in Edison Township, was formerly a United States government reservation.

RED LION (RED TAVERN), in North Brunswick Township, was founded before 1800 and derives its name from a tavern that was once a center of life here.

REDSHAW CORNER, in Madison Township, owes its origin in all probability to the Redshaw family, early settlers. Old residents say the place was also called "Paint House Corner."

RHODE HALL, in East and South Brunswick Townships, derives its name from the ancestral home in Scotland of David Williamson, a leader among the

152

Scottish families who settled more than two centuries ago in this area. Rhode Hall was obviously an inn. A race course, known as the Rhode Hall Driving Park, also operated near here at one time.

RUNYON, in Madison Township, recalls those sturdy French Huguenots named Roignon [later Runyon, Runyan], who came to New Jersey about 1665. Three years later Philip Carteret, governor of East Jersey, issued a license for the marriage of Vincent Roignon to Ann Boutcher.

SAND HILLS, in South Brunswick Township, takes its name from "noted" hills hereabouts.

SAYREVILLE, once known as "Roundabout" because it could only be reached by a twisting journey over the Raritan and South rivers, was formed as a township from South Amboy on April 6, 1876. By then the area had been settled for at least a hundred years, and the first land probably was "taken up" as early as 1683. The present name, adopted in 1872, honors James R. Sayre, Jr., an extensive landowner and manufacturer. See also *Ernston, Morgan, Parlin, South Amboy.*

SCHALKS, in Plainsboro Township, probably owes its name to Herman and Caroline Schalk of Newark, early owners of property in this region. When the railroad station was built, about 1870, no Schalk owned property in the vicinity, but the old name was retained.

SCOTTS CORNER, in Plainsboro Township, honors Dr. Moses Scott, a pre-Revolutionary settler.

153

SEWAREN, in Woodbridge Township, was established as a station or "post village" on the Long Branch division of the Pennsylvania and Reading Railroad.

SOUTH AMBOY became a township in 1685. Originally covering an area of 64,000 acres, part of its territory was given to Monroe Township in 1838, part to Madison Township in 1869, and part to Sayreville in 1876. The borough of South Amboy was established in 1888. An early name was "Radford's," and probably referred to Andrew Radford (Redford), who operated a private ferry here in connection with the road built between Perth Amboy and Burlington. See Chapter I.

SOUTH BRUNSWICK TOWNSHIP derived its impetus from the many taverns that made it a key point on one of the busiest stagecoach routes in New Jersey. A portion of the township's area was given to Cranbury in 1872. There was evidence of an early Indian encampment when Jediah Higgins became a settler in 1700. See also *Dayton, Deans, Franklin Park, Fresh Ponds, Kingston, Little Rocky Hill, Monmouth Junction, Sand Hills, Ten Mile Run.*

SOUTH PLAINFIELD was settled about 1685. Earlier names for this vicinity were "New Brooklyn" (from Brooklyn, Connecticut), "Samptown" (perhaps from the word "samp," meaning a coarse hominy), and "Towtown."

SOUTH RIVER, which became a borough in 1897-98, has been described as "what was formerly part of the village of Washington." Its beginning dates back to Hartshorne Willet (or Samuel Willett) about 1720, when the place was known for a time as "Willettstown."

SPOTSWOOD probably received its name from John Lewis Johnston, an early settler descended from the ancient family of "Spottiswoode in Scotland." Originally the town's name was spelled with two *t*'s. It was known as a manufacturing point by 1750, and perhaps before; iron was manufactured here before the Revolution, and there was a paper mill by the time that war started. The present borough was created on April 15, 1908. See also *Outcalt*.

STELTON, in Edison Township, derives its name from the Stelles, a family of French Huguenots who settled in this neighborhood in the late 17th century. At one time it was called "Baptist Crossing" and "Baptist Roads."

TEN MILE RUN, in South Brunswick Township, takes its name from the fact that it is ten miles south of New Brunswick on the old road to Princeton.

TEXAS, in Monroe Township, was early settled by a Tice and Peter Mount. A "Little Texas" was a Negro settlement in Freehold. Old residents remember hearing the place referred to as "Mill Bridge."

UNION VALLEY, in Monroe Township, derives its name as the intersecting point for a number of roads. A roadside marker indicates the site of the Union Valley Methodist Protestant Church, erected in 1790. See *Old Church*.

WESTONS MILLS, on Lawrence Brook in New Brunswick

155

may have been the site of a mill as early as 1716.

WOODBRIDGE, chartered as a township June 1, 1669, was named for the Reverend John Woodbridge, who was born in Wiltshire, England, settled in Massachusetts and led a number of families into this area during the summer of 1665. See also *Avenel, Colonia, Edgar, Fords, Iselin, Keasbey, Port Reading, Sewaren,* and Chapter I.

WYCKOFF'S MILLS, in Cranbury Township, takes its name from an old gristmill on the Millstone River owned by Peter Wyckoff, an early settler of Cranbury.

B. BY OTHER NAMES, LARGELY FORGOTTEN

Abraham's Ford—Washington [South River]
Allentown—Metuchen
Anabaptist Town—Piscataway
Aqueduct Mill—Gray's Mills
Arbor—Piscataway
Bald Hill—Woodbridge [settled 1689 by the Reverend Archibald Riddell of Scotland]
Baptist Crossing, Baptist Roads—Stelton
Barcla's [Barclett's] Point—Perth Amboy [given or patented in 1687 to Thomas Bartlett (Barclett) and described as "over against Perth Amboy"]
Bergen's Mill—Milltown
Bethel—Monroe Township [an Indian town near present-day Jamesburg established when David Brainerd brought his Indian mission here from Cross-

wick in 1746. About 120 Indians, converted to the Christian faith, followed Brainerd to Bethel.]

Blondyn Plains—New Market

Bloomfield Mills—possibly Helmetta

Blue Hills—Piscataway

Bodine's Corners—Berdines Corners

Bridgetown—Colonia

Brunson—North Brunswick Township [once the site of a tavern]

Buckelew's Mills—Jamesburg

Burt's Creek—Sayreville Township [once famous for its greenhouses]

Caldonia—Jamesburg, Metuchen [Perth Amboy had a "Caldonian Park"]

Campbell's Gully—Perth Amboy [the Campbell brothers, exiles from Scotland, held lots in a ravine north of the town]

Chaqusitt—Cheesequake [Indian name]

Cole Point—Perth Amboy

Cross Roads—Dayton

Cutler's Mill—Perth Amboy

Demarest [Demorest]—Avenel [also "Demarest on the Hilltop"]

Devil's Half Acre—Half Acre

Endsley's [Ensley's] Mills—Jamesburg

"Falls of the Raritan"—Highland Park [Indian name]

Florida Grove—Keasbey [site of a famous clay-bed outcropping]

Florida Landing—Perth Amboy [a landmark in colonial times]

Gordon's Mills—Jamesburg

Gray's Mills—Aqueduct [probably named for Alexander Gray. The name also is spelled "Grey's Mill." The mill itself was pre-Revolutionary and due to its proximity to the aqueduct that carried the Delaware and Raritan Canal over the Millstone River, it was sometimes called "Aqueduct Mill."]

Green Brook—Middlesex Borough

Hardenburg Corners—East Brunswick Township

Herbertsville—Old Bridge

Hoffman—Monroe Township [a flag-station on the Freehold Railroad]

Houghtenville [Houtenville]—Colonia

"Indian Fields"—South Brunswick Township [site of an Indian encampment]

Inian's Ferry [Inian's Ford]—New Brunswick

Jacksonville—Cheesequake

Leestown—Woodbridge Township [derives its name from the Lee family who were early settlers in the region. Once called "Leesville."]

Lincoln Gardens—New Brunswick [annexed to the city in 1909]

Livingston Park—North Brunswick Township [a small hamlet on the Trenton and New Brunswick Turnpike, now Livingston Avenue; it recalls William Livingston, first governor after New Jersey acquired statehood and through whose efforts in 1787 the State passed an act forbidding the importation of slaves]

Longfield's Mills—Westons Mills

Mapletown—Maple Meade

Martinsville—Deans

Matchaponix—Texas [Indian name]

Mechanicsville—Sayreville [a small settlement once bordering on South Amboy]

Mile Run—North Brunswick Township [so called because it was one mile south of New Brunswick]

Mill Bridge—Texas

Milton—Colonia

New Brooklyn—South Plainfield

Paint House Corner—Redshaw Corner

Perrytown—Iselin

Pigeon Swamp—Fresh Ponds

Pocohant—Avenel [Indian name]

Pridmore's [Prigmore's] Swamp—New Brunswick

Quibbletown—New Market

Radford's [Redford's]—South Amboy

Randolphville—Newtown

Raritan Landing—Piscataway [at the head of the tidewater, two miles above New Brunswick where a wooden bridge crossed the river, once a place of considerable activity]

Raritan Township—Edison Township

Red Tavern [Red Lion]—Applegarth

Roosevelt—Carteret

Rossell's Mills—Jamesburg

Roundabout—Sayreville

Samptown—South Plainfield

Sand Hills—Fords [South Brunswick]

Sandy Run—Deans

Sheppard's Landing—Washington

Six Mile Run—South Brunswick Township [a stop on the post road twelve miles from Princeton and four from New Brunswick. The village took its name from the brook which was approximately six miles long.]

Slingtail Crossing—Fords

Spring Valley—Applegarth

Squabbletown—New Market

Tanners Corner—East Brunswick

Three Mile Run—North Brunswick Township [site of an Old Dutch Reformed Church, probably the oldest Christian church south of the Raritan]

Towtown—South Plainfield

Tracy—Monroe Township [a flag-station on the Freehold Railroad]

Uniontown—Iselin

Warne's Bridge—Madison Township [honors Thomas Warne, a carpenter and son of a Dublin merchant who came to Spotswood late in the 17th century]

Washington—South River [once a busy shipping center for wood, grain and peaches. A steamboat route connected New York and Washington, whence a stage-coach line carried passengers and freight to the Delaware at Bordentown, but this service ended in 1832 when the Camden and Amboy Railroad was completed as far as Hightstown.]

Waterville—New Market

Weechqueechley—Outcalt

West [West's] Turnout—Jamesburg

Wigwam Grove—Monroe Township
Willettstown—South River
Woodside [Woodville]—Fresh Ponds

Acknowledgments

Many selfless friends have contributed of their wisdom and faith to the writing of this book.

Foremost among this group is Dr. William H. Cole, who first conceived of *Where the Raritan Flows* and persuaded me to write it.

Special indebtedness also is due the Board of Freeholders of Middlesex County, who supported the project from its inception and never once dictated how a single word should be written.

In the same spirit, the advisory committee appointed by the Freeholders gave the author freedom in writing as he thought best, and it is with pleasure that I acknowledge my gratitude to these gentlemen: the

Honorable William Kurtz, member of the General Assembly; Dr. Roy Franklin Nichols, vice-provost and dean of the Graduate School of Arts and Science, University of Pennsylvania; Dr. Mason Gross, president, Rutgers University; Dr. Robert R. Blunt, superintendent of schools, Middlesex County; Karl E. Metzger, former director, Middlesex County Board of Freeholders; Dr. Richard P. McCormick, professor of history, Rutgers University; and Louis P. Booz, consulting engineer and affectionate historian of Perth Amboy.

No one can ever work in any phase of New Jersey history without thankfulness for the presence of Donald A. Sinclair, custodian of the New Jersey collections in the Rutgers University Library, and I am one of a faithful legion eager to attest to that fact. Among the many others who gave special encouragement to this work were Mr. Alex Eber of New Brunswick, Mr. Joseph T. Karcher of Sayreville, and Messrs. Charles H. Reed and William Shelley of New Brunswick.

I am especially happy to repeat, as I have done once in "What's in a Name," my particular debt to William Miller of the History Department of Rutgers University for the research assistance that he gave to specific parts of this work. The manuscript also was read by Professor Hubert G. Schmidt.

All these wonderful persons—and many others who deserve to be listed—share one truth in common: in no way are they responsible for any error in the preceding pages.

E. S. M.

Index

Note: For derivation of specific place names, see alphabetical listing in chapter entitled, "What's in a Name?", pp. 135–61.

Bedloe's Island, N. Y., 64
Bell, Alexander Graham, 108
Bellona, the, 59, 60
Bennet's Island, 37
Bergen, 6
Bergen County, 6, 8
Bergen, Jacob I., 148
Bey, Abraham, 130
"Big Mike," 96–7, 98. *See also*
    Michael, J.
Bishop, John, 11
Bishop, Rebecca, 12
Blauvelt, Abraham, 128
Bloomfield, Thomas, 11
Bodine, Nicholas, 138
Bonham, Nicholas, 138
Bonhamtown, 42
Bordentown, 126
Bound Brook, 40, 48, 54, 68
Boutcher, Ann, 153
Bradford, William, 21
Bradley, Joseph P., 95
Brainerd, David, 150–1
Brandywine, Pa., 43
Bristol, Pa., 7
British Army: occupies New
    Brunswick, 34; losses dur-
    ing Revolution, 38; cam-
    paign against New Bruns-
    wick, 41; ends occupation
    of N. J., 42–3; march to
    New York, 43–4
Brookford Snuff Mills, 125–6
Brown, H. F., 151

Brown, Jacob, 88
Brown, John and Susannah,
    138
Brunswick Gazette, 128
Buckelew, Frederick, 143
Buckelew, James, 143
Buford, Col. Abraham, 48
Burlington, 7, 18, 43, 50

Camden and Amboy Rail-
    road, 60, 77, 126
Campbell, Dr. William H.,
    100
Carteret, Lord Philip, 14, 153
Centennial Exposition, 108
Charlotte, Queen Consort of
    England, 91
Chatham, 54
Chesapeake Bay, 53
Clermont, the, 57
Clinton, George, Governor of
    N. Y., 54
Clinton, Sir Henry, 43, 44, 48
Coetus, the, 90
College of New Jersey, 90
Combs, Samuel, 142
Conferentie, the, 90
Conger, John, 88–9
Continental Army: retreat
    through N. J., 33; encoun-
    ter with Howe near New
    Market, 42; march to Vir-
    ginia, 54–5; victory at York-

tablished, 8; early settlers, 11, 12, 13; first printing for, 21; as bellwether of Revolution, 22; resistance to Stamp Act, 25; Committees of Correspondence, 26; resistance to Parliament, 26; prepares for war, 27; food and dress during Revolutionary era, 29, 32; Revolutionary raiders, 50; colonial schools, 88–9; industrial development, 118–31; 18th century tavern rates, 120–1; 18th century industry, 119, 121; 19th century industry, 124; snuff mills, 125–6; economic growth from 1794–1831, 124–5; coming of railroad, 126–7; newspapers, 128; present day industry, 130–1, mentioned, 4, 35, 37, 42, 43, 44, 78, 105

Middletown, 8
Millstone, 41, 91
Milltown, 128
Mine Gully, 108, 117
Minisink Island, 5
Minisink Path, 4–5
Monmouth, Battle of, 44
Monmouth County, 8
Monmouth Court House (Freehold), 44

Monroe, President James, 148
Moore, Mathew, 12
Morris, Lewis, 149
Morristown, 35, 36, 40
Mount, Tice and Peter, 155

Napoleon Company of New Brunswick, 64
Nassau Hall, 35
Navesink, 4
Neilson, Col. John, 28, 32, 33, 34, 37
New American Magazine, 21
New Amstel (New Castle), Del., 6
New Amsterdam, N. Y., 6, 7
Newark, 5, 8
New Brunswick: Albany St., 19, 20; early settlers, 18–19; early description of, 19, 20, 22; Liberty Boys, 23–4; pre-Revolutionary scuffles, 24–5; setting for anti-British conference, 26; copy of Declaration of Independence arrives in, 28; British attack, 33; British occupation of, 34, 37; losses to British raiders, 38; celebrates second anniversary of 4th of July, 45; "Washington's Headquarters," 50; British attack Hyler's raiders, 53; steamboat ferry

170

service, 57, 58, 59; Napoleon Company of, 64; visited by Lincoln, 77–8; Dutch settlers, 89–90; proposed as site for university, 91; recommended as N. J. state capital, 121, 124; 19th century industry, 124; wallpaper industry, 127; rubber industry, 127–8; newspapers, 128; mentioned, 7, 27, 35, 36, 41, 42, 44, 48, 49, 50, 51, 54, 66, 91, 130, 131

New Brunswick Fredonian, 128

New Brunswick Steamboat Ferry Company, 60

New Brunswick Times and General Advertiser, 128

New Castle, Del., 6, 7. *See also* New Amstel

Newell, William A., 95

New Jersey: Dutch settlement in, 6; division into counties, 8; Revolutionary War in, 23–55; vs. New York in steamboat wars, 57; steamboat legislation, 58

New Market, 13, 24, 42, 48, 90

New Philadelphia, the, 60, 64

New Utrecht, N. Y., 51

New York: trade with New Brunswick, 20; as British base, 43; vs. N. J. in steamboat wars, 57; ferry service to N. J., 58, 59; mentioned, 53, 54, 65, 116

New York and Harlem Railroad, 126

Nixon, Col. Lewis, 150

Noordt River (Hudson), 6

North Branch, 91

North Brunswick, 125

Olive Branch, the, 59

Outcalt, John D., 151

Oyster Bay, N. Y., 86

Paine, Thomas, 39

Parker, James, 21

Parlin, 131–2

Patten, Abraham, 41

Pelzer, Hubert and Alfonso, 145, 148

Pennsylvania Railroad, 111

Perkins, "Daddy," 151

Perth Amboy: early settlement by Scotch, 14–15; attacked by Simcoe's raiders, 48, 49; as site of Solomon Andrew's experiments, 73; British printing restrictions on, 89; present day industry in, 130–1, 132; mentioned, 18, 21, 25, 70, 71, 86, 87, 105, 127, 129

Perth Amboy Steamboat Company, 64

Philadelphia, Pa., vi, 26, 43

Philadelphia, Germantown and Norristown Railroad, 126

Phoenix, the, 57, 58

Physical Culture, 151

Pierce, Daniel, 11

Piscataway: 17th century settlement, 13; losses inflicted by British raids, 38; first school, 89; present day industry in, 131; mentioned, 7, 8, 18, 26, 42

Plainsboro, 131

Pluckemin, 48

Plumb, C. M., 85

Political Intelligencer, 128

Port Jervis, N. Y., 5

Port Reading, 131

Potter, James R., 152

Prickett, Josiah, 139

Pridmore's (Prigmore's) Swamp, 18. *See also* New Brunswick

Princeton, 7, 34, 41, 42, 43, 69

Princeton, Battle of, 35

Princeton University: Nassau Hall, 35; participant in first football game, 96–8; cannon war with Rutgers, 98–102; mentioned, 94

Pumptown, 116

Punishments, colonial, 10, 11, 12, 21, 24, 25

Putnam, Gen. Israel, 41

Queens College, 91. *See also* Rutgers

Quibbletown, 13. *See also* New Market

Radford (Redford), Andrew, 154

Rahway River, 4

Randolph, John Fitz, 149–50

Randolph, Thomas, 24

Raritan, the, 58, 60, 61, 64

Raritan River: steamboat wars, 56, 58–60; 19th century travel on, 64–5; present day life along, 70; as setting for Rutgers, 95–6; mentioned, 4, 7, 8, 33, 44, 50, 52

Raritan Township, 117. *See also* Edison Township

Revolutionary War, 23–55

River wars, 56, 58–60, 64

Roads, colonial, 6–7

Robison, John, 21

Roignon, Vincent, 153

Rutgers, Col. Henry, 94

Rutgers, the State University: 90–105; role in Civil War, 79; charter, 91; first classes,